PRACTICAL SOCIAL WORK

Series Editor: Jo Campling

BASW

Editorial Advisory Board:
Robert Adams, Terry Bamford, Charles Barker, Lena Dominelli,
Malcolm Payne, Michael Preston-Shoot, Daphne Statham
and Jane Tunstill

Social work is at an important stage in its development. All professions must be responsive to changing social and economic conditions if they are to meet the needs of those they serve. This series focuses on sound practice and the specific contribution which social workers can make to the well-being of our society.

The British Association of Social Workers has always been conscious of its role in setting guidelines for practice and in seeking to raise professional standards. The conception of the Practical Social Work series arose from a survey of BASW members to discover where they, the practitioners in social work, felt there was the most need for new literature. The response was overwhelming and enthusiastic, and the result is a carefully planned, coherent series of books. The emphasis is firmly on practice set in a theoretical framework. The books will inform, stimulate and promote discussion, thus adding to the further development of skills and high professional standards. All the authors are practitioners and teachers of social work representing a wide variety of experience.

JO CAMPLING

A list of published titles in this series follows overleaf

PRACTICAL SOCIAL WORK

Communication in Social Work

Joyce Lishman

MACMILLAN

First published 1994 by
THE MACMILLAN PRESS LTD
Houndmills, Basingstoke, Hampshire RG21 2XS
and London
Companies and representatives
throughout the world

ISBN 0–333–54411–0 hardcover
ISBN 0–333–54412–9 paperback

A catalogue record for this book is available
from the British Library.

Printed in Hong Kong

To Roly, Tamsin and Benjamin for their love, support and encouragement over many years

Contents

Acknowledgements

In preparing this book I have drawn on knowledge, wisdom, expertise and support from colleagues, students and clients – past and present – and wish to acknowledge their contributions to my own development, learning and understanding. I owe particular appreciation to Gerard Rochford, my PhD supervisor and mentor, Molly Russell, for efficient manuscript typing, and Roly Lishman, for emotional support, word processing and referencing.

JOYCE LISHMAN

1

Introduction

Effective communication is an essential component of traditional social work activities, e.g. providing basic care, giving advice, making assessments, counselling, writing reports and acting as clients' advocates. It is equally necessary for social workers to have effective communication skills if they are to promote self-help and empowerment. Finally, while the language of community care planning, with its emphasis on care management, brokerage, the purchaser/provider split and devolved budgets sounds technocratic and impersonal, care managers and providers will have to use a range of communication and interpersonal skills if community care is really to mean care, choice and empowerment for users.

I am also aware that the major problems facing social work are those of poverty and discrimination or oppression on the basis of race, class, gender, age and disability. Any amelioration or solution requires political and structural change. However social workers, in general, are faced with the impact of structural problems on individuals and families and the need to engage in direct interaction requires the use of the range of communication skills examined in this volume.

One reason for wanting to write this book, therefore, was because communication skills are at the core of social work. A second reason was that understanding and knowledge about effective communication is derived from a variety of sources, e.g. social psychology, evaluation research, social work theory, and research into clients' perceptions of social work: the range of knowledge requires integration and application to social work. A third reason is that while training in social work acknowledges the importance of communication skills, our knowledge about their use in real practice is very limited. Partly this is because in many settings, particularly fieldwork and secondary settings, social work is an 'invisible' profession, practised in private and unobserved (Pithouse, 1987). Partly it is because few research studies have examined, even descriptively, workers' behaviour and interaction with clients

1

(Baldock and Prior, 1981; Lishman, 1985), let alone attempted to evaluate the effectiveness of different communication techniques and styles.

My aims in this volume are:

- to draw together the knowledge we have from different sources about the communication skills we need for effective social work practice and to present these in a clear available way
- to apply this knowledge to social work in a range of contexts and settings

Consider the following two social workers. The first is interviewing a female client who referred herself to her GP because she was anxious that she was punishing her 7-year-old son excessively. In interview the social worker's voice is gentle and soft. She appears attentive and listens carefully. She checks out that she has understood what the client is saying. She smiles frequently, her face is expressive and she appears warm, interested and sympathetic. Her responses are supportive to her client and she reinforces positive behaviour on the client's part, e.g. 'Don't play it down. Aren't you pleased to have managed that?' She clarifies what the client says, and shows verbally that she is understanding her.

In contrast a worker is interviewing a young man who is on probation to her, and who has just re-offended by serious housebreaking. In interview the social worker's voice sounds rather cold and harsh. She fidgets and moves about rather impatiently as if she has heard it all before. She does not smile and her face is impassive and serious: her only facial expression is to frown. She questions in quite an abrupt way 'Well, what was it about, then?' and rejects the answer, 'I know it was about house-breaking but...'. She does not appear supportive and does not check out her understanding of the client. Her responses are often critical and she confronts the probationer with her scepticism about his future behaviour and ability to stay out of prison.

Two very different clients with different problems and agendas. Two different interviews and two different communication styles on the part of the worker. Interestingly, the social worker is the same person! She was filmed interviewing these two clients as part of a study (Lishman, 1985) which explored and analysed social workers' behaviour in interviews. Social work students and educators, social workers and health visitors who have watched the tapes have found it difficult to believe the worker was the same person.

The interviews are described because they raise central questions about communication in social work. What skills are used? Do the skills used change in response to the client? Does a social worker use the same skills regardless of client or problem? Can we say that individual social workers have individual communication styles? The answers to these questions are descriptive. We need also to ask what communication skills are effective and more specifically what communication skills are effective in what settings, with what clients and for what purposes? These questions are evaluative.

The answers, in so far as there are answers, are drawn from a range of sources. Social psychology can help us to understand the meaning and interpretation of our non-verbal and symbolic behaviour, the relevance of class, race and gender to verbal communication, and influences on interpersonal perception, such as stereotyping. Behavioural theory reminds us of the importance of reinforcement and modelling.

Research into clients' perceptions gives us clear feedback about social workers' communication skills or lack of them. Evaluative research in social work, psychotherapy and counselling highlights the importance of the worker showing empathy, warmth and genuineness, the 'core conditions' for effective helping, and of the use of contract-based intervention and focused intervention methods such as task-centred work.

Practice theory in social work confidently prescribes how we *ought* to behave and communicate. Unfortunately the evidence to support such prescription is more limited. 'Much has been written about what social workers should *know* and *be* and *believe in* and hope to *achieve* but the work itself, the technical moves by which we distinguish ourselves from other professions, are undefined' (Schwartz, 1973). In this book I draw upon practice theory, even where it has not been rigorously researched, provided it is supported by collective practice experience and evidence from relevant sources such as social psychology or evaluation research.

I draw on my own practice experience and what I have learned from my students because I believe a book which claims to be relevant to practice has to have a firm practice base. I also believe that practice experience and wisdom must contribute to the development of knowledge and theory in social work.

This book, in drawing on all these sources, applies them to social work practice. I begin in Chapter 2 with our clients' views on what constitutes helpful and effective communication. Like Wallace and Rees (1984), I would argue that clients' judgements are 'the most important criterion' (p.58) in evaluating social work and the personal social services. Wallace and Rees believe that social workers' accountability to clients should take 'precedence over accountability to agency or profession' (p.58) and that in response to clients' problems which are largely structural 'social workers' responsibility is never to lose sight of the needs of the most powerless people' (p.58). This must involve seeking and actively responding to their perceptions and evaluations.

The next chapter examines different kinds of communication: symbolic, non-verbal, verbal and written. Symbolic communication involves aspects of our behaviour and presentation, such as punctuality, dress, the kind of food we provide in residential care, and the kind of basic care we give, which convey a symbolic as well as literal message to our clients, e.g. about our respect and care for them or about the power relationship between us. Non-verbal communication is precisely that; not spoken communication but communication through behaviour such as facial expression, gaze, orientation and body movement.

Verbal communication is what we say and includes questioning, reflection, focusing, summarising, challenging and confrontation. Verbal communication involves the use of language, and we need to be aware that worker and client may not share the same language. Interpretation, with its implications for clear communication, may be necessary.

Subsequent chapters apply different kinds of communication to different purposes of social work. Chapter 4 examines relationship building and maintaining and the skills of conveying genuineness, warmth, acceptance, encouragement, empathy and responsiveness, Chapter 5 examines the skills involved in attending and listening, including the use of silence. Chapter 6 is about sharing information: getting information, by using reflection, paraphrasing, clarification, questioning and probing, and giving information and advice in either verbal or written form. Chapter 7 examines the use of contracts and the skills involved: summarising, focusing and negotiation. Finally Chapters 8 and 9 examine intervention skills and means of helping clients achieve change in attitudes or behaviour. Here we are concerned with the use of influence, both with skills like questioning, probing, advising summarising and focusing, examined previously, and with new skills such as interpretation and confrontation. The final chapter concludes with a summary of guidelines for effective communication.

The skills identified and examined throughout the book are transferable skills. They are applicable across a range of settings, including group care, fieldwork and secondary settings, and to a range of client groups, including children, older people, people with learning difficult-ies, people with mental health problems and people with disabilities. I hope that I adequately acknowledge the implications of class, gender and ethnicity for effective communication.

Perhaps the major limitation of the volume is that its focus is on social workers' communication with clients or service users, and does not explicitly include their communication with colleagues, either from social work or from other disciplines. However the skills involved in engaging, listening, negotiating and challenging are equally relevant to communication in work groups and multidisciplinary teams. I hope that readers will find the examination and discussion of skills applicable not only to clients, but transferable to wider communication in their work setting.

Finally, *writing* about communication is inevitably limited and problem-atic. Communication is an activity which has to be performed and prac-tised. In order to develop skills, feedback has to be sought and acted upon. The reader is therefore invited first to consider and reflect on the discussion in this volume, but also, and more importantly, to use and practice the skills identified, and to seek feedback on them from clients, colleagues or video, in order to develop further competence in using them.

2

Helpful and Effective Communication : Our Clients' Views

Mayer and Timms (1970) first highlighted the importance and complete neglect of seeking clients' views about the social work services they received. The growth of studies of clients' opinions since then reflects a developing recognition that clients are consumers of social work and should have some voice in its appraisal and development. Any commitment to the empowerment of social work clients is meaningless if their views are neither sought nor taken into account, although in residential work we still know little of clients' or residents' views, because, as Booth (1983) suggests 'surprisingly little effort has been made to find out' (p. 24).

While clients are not a homogeneous group who will speak with one voice, Rees and Wallace's (1982) review of the literature on clients' evaluations of social work does identify common themes. Rees and Wallace distinguished between client *satisfaction* relating to the worker's style of response or perceived helpfulness, and client *evaluation* based on the outcome of contact and its effectiveness. This distinction can be made in terms of communication.

What kinds of communication were perceived by clients as being helpful?

Helpful communication

Clients coming for social work help are likely to be bewildered, confused and ignorant about social work. They frequently arrive at a social work agency with a sense of stigma or shame, and suspicious, hostile or fearful expectations. Davies (1985) reminds us of the 'grim determination' needed by a client 'to cross the agency threshold'. Many clients come in a crisis when they are likely to be particularly sensitive to their first point of contact, reception.

Hall (1974) investigating reception in children's departments, observed receptionists who appeared unsympathetic to clients and asked them to discuss personal problems in front of a waiting-room of clients. Such a reception was perceived as insensitive, disinterested and devaluing. More generally, as Davies (1985) argues, the literature on client perceptions indicates the need for greater sensitivity, individualisation and tact on the part of social work receptionists.

From the social worker, clients initially appreciated warmth, informality and friendliness. They valued social workers who showed personal concern and interest and did not seem to be 'just doing a job'. As Davies (1985) suggests, client studies show that 'the true professional is not someone who is cool, detached, career-minded and disinterested' but is someone who shows friendliness, understanding and warmth in a way which convinces the client of his/her concern.

Clients saw this concern as communicated if the worker expressed interest about their families, activities or hobbies, or was prepared to visit outside office hours (Sainsbury, 1975; Gottesfield, 1965). Lack of concern was communicated, according to clients, by the worker appearing bored or inattentive, e.g. staring out of the window when the client was talking (Reith 1975), keeping clients waiting (Hoffman, 1975) or breaking appointments at the last minute.

Clients valued social workers who listened attentively. Clients whose daughter had died very suddenly appreciated 'having someone outside the family just to sit and listen' (Lishman *et al.*, 1990). This act of listening is often valued in itself, independent of other help given. Patience and an unhurried approach are also appreciated by clients. Again this conveys a personal concern, individualisation and acknowledgement of the importance of the client's concerns; 'I was quite surprised they had time to bother because they've lots of people to deal with and maybe my case, it was big to me, but it was quite trivial to them' (Rees, 1974, p.259).

Some clients, arriving at a social work agency, have ambivalent or negative feelings about asking for help. Clients seeking material or financial help felt a sense of stigma or shame at having to ask for help (Mayer and Timms, 1970). Clients who had to ask for practical or care services experienced this as demeaning. Clients who felt ashamed or apprehensive valued social workers who were able to put them at their ease. How did social workers help clients to feel more at ease? Rees and Wallace (1982) stress the importance of the social worker enabling the client to ask for help, especially by anticipating potential requests and putting them into words. This involves the worker in being sensitive to the client's feelings of shame and alert to potential needs and requests. Social workers stressing clients' entitlement to money was helpful, whereas stressing the cost of the help or shortage of resources increased clients' feeling of shame and dependence (Blaxter, 1976; Sainsbury, 1975).

Where clients felt anxious or ashamed about seeking help with interpersonal problems, they appreciated an individualised and friendly reception, patient, attentive listening and understanding. They emphasised the importance of a non-judgemental approach (Silverman, 1969; Jackson, 1973; Orlinsky and Howard, 1967). Although they realised that social workers had to ask questions they appreciated a non-intrusive approach. Rees and Wallace (1982, p.32) suggest that 'too many questions, too early in contact can at times only confirm a client's suspicion that he or she is being judged or cross-examined'.

A client may be anxious about the authority and power of the agency. While authority is inherent in the role of social work some fears may be unrealistic. A client at a child and family psychiatry clinic exemplifies this: 'I was frightened. I thought they would say I was a bad mother and take him away from me. When they took him away (to see a psychiatrist while she saw a social worker) I wondered where he was going. I did not ask' (Lishman, 1978). I was the social worker and was unaware at the time of this intense anxiety. For me the initial encounter was a regular everyday experience. For my client it was unique and I should have been more aware of her anxiety and conveyed my recognition of it.

While warmth, empathy, patient listening and a non-judgemental approach were important to clients, they did not necessarily overcome clients' negative perceptions of social work and social work agencies. A client might trust an individual worker but remain suspicious of the agency. The client would perceive the worker as atypical: Sainsbury and Nixon (1979) found that most of the clients in their study saw the social worker as more positive and caring than the agency from which they came.

Finally clients found activity by the social worker helpful. Rees and Wallace (1982) suggest 'By 'doing things' or attempting to do things social workers confirm their concern and willingness to help.' Activity includes advice-giving, and making arrangements on behalf of clients. Such activities have not always been valued in the social work literature: for example, advice-giving has been seen as contradicting the principle of client self-determination (Biestek, 1965) and making arrangements on behalf of clients as encouraging the client's dependence. Clients do not appear to share these reservations, e.g. one client gave the following reasons for finding his social worker helpful 'he gave advice about social security, would go along to court or write a letter – I don't have to stammer out to someone who has no sympathy' (Lishman, 1985). Activity is appreciated by clients even if it is unsuccessful. For example, Jackson (1973) found in a study of long-term work with multi-problem families that what seemed important was the effort the social workers made on their behalf and not its effectiveness.

Effective communication

Because some communication and behaviour is perceived as *helpful* by clients it does not mean it is *effective* in terms of achieving a desired outcome. Maluccio (1979) argues that while warmth and friendliness may initially give clients a sense of hope and raise their expectations, if the expectations are subsequently not met clients may feel let down. Maluccio suggests that different qualities and skills may be required at different stages: warmth and sympathy initially, competence and knowledge later.

What do clients see as contributing to social workers' effectiveness? Clients stress knowledge and expertise, use of authority, agreement between client and worker about the purpose of contact, acceptance of the client's need to unburden, a task-centred approach and provision of advice and material help.

Three main areas of knowledge and experience were valued by clients (Rees and Wallace, 1982):

1. Clients valued workers who had enough experience of life to listen non-judgementally to what might appear shocking aspects of their lives, for example, violence, deprivation, loss or deviance. A non-judgemental attitude is not synonymous with condoning destructive, anti-social or sadistic behaviour, but if a social worker, because of limited life experience or a limited awareness of the range of human behavior, expresses shock, disapproval, or a kind of salacious over-inquisitiveness, any basis for effective work by client and worker is lost.

2. Clients valued workers who had enough life experience to understand clients' problems from their own experience. For example, experience of marriage or parenthood was seen as important if the client's situation involved child-rearing, marital or family problems. Age was important: clients frequently expressed dissatisfaction with young social workers. 'He was just a young lad. He wasn't old enough to understand my problem properly' (Reich, 1975). More specifically clients valued social workers who acknowledged they had had similar problems and surmounted them: this gave clients hope that the problems were not insoluble (Rees and Wallace, 1982).

3. Clients appreciated specialised knowledge and training, or rather criticised workers for lack of specialised knowledge. In particular, parents of children who were physically or mentally handicapped complained about workers' lack of knowledge of the handicap itself and of relevant benefits and facilities (Butler; 1977; Robinson; 1978; Rees and Wallace, 1982).

Clearly age and life experience are not aspects of self which an individual social worker can change. How can we apply these findings? First, it is important that a young social worker is aware that her/his youth may initially be perceived as a handicap by the client. Second, being young does not mean being naive or easily shockable.Young workers can use training to examine their own attitudes to a range of 'shocking' situations and thereby to widen (almost prematurely) their life experience. Third, no individual social worker can have direct experience of all problematic life experiences. The need for transferability of understanding and knowledge, e.g. of loss, abuse, oppression or discrimination is necessary across client groups and individual problem situations. Finally all social workers have to take responsibility for the continuing development of specialised knowledge. The achievement of such expertise is likely to compensate for youth, but, more importantly, is essential for effective work with particular client groups. This does not imply that a social worker needs to know everything a client might ask: rather that she or he 'has a responsibility to have at her/his fingertips detailed, accurate and up-to-date knowledge about the law, welfare rights and local community facilities, and be willing to turn for help to others in the agency' (Davies, 1985, p.25). Social workers need to be able to say honestly 'I don't know' but such a statement should imply a responsibility to find out and feed back the information to the client.

Appropriate use of power and authority is an essential component of effectiveness as perceived by clients but appropriate use is perceived differently by different clients. Some clients appreciated a relationship based on equality with the social worker in problem-sharing, and did not wish the social worker to exercise power and control over them. Such clients had what Rees and Wallace (1982, p.39) called 'an orientation to problem-solving'. 'Most of the people in this group have had past experience of dealing with officials and feel fairly confident in dealing with social workers, many are well educated, and, enjoying a certain degree of economic security, they have a sense of control over their lives. For them, 'the social worker is an expert and an ally to be consulted...' (Rees and Wallace, 1982). This preference appears to be found most often, perhaps unsurprisingly, among foster parents and parents of children with physical handicaps or learning difficulties.

In contrast, other clients preferred the social worker to be directive and exercise authority over them. According to Rees and Wallace (1982) such clients tended to be poor, to experience themselves as having little control over their lives and to have had past experience of people in authority which led them to 'assume a relationship of unequal power and knowledge. The social worker is the expert whom it is inappropriate to challenge' (p.41).

For such clients effective power and authority is exercised in two ways: by advice and guidance, and by control and limit setting. Some clients perceive the social worker as more effective the more advice is given. They expect that after they have told the social worker their problems some kind of diagnosis and solution will be given and if it is not 'the clients feel somewhat let down and disappointed' (Rees and Wallace, 1982). Some clients appreciate the social worker exercising authority over them by being firm, for example, by instructing them to carry out certain tasks, demanding certain behaviour or giving strong guidance (Sainsbury, 1975). 'They've got to be strong. They should be able to take control of the situation' (Sainsbury, 1975).

Other clients, particularly parents, wish the social worker to exercise control over others, their children. Fisher *et al.* (1986) commenting on parents' passive acceptance of loss of authority over their children, suggest 'if difficulties had reached the point where a parent could not exercise proper authority over the child, it was logical in the parents' eyes to exercise responsibility by calling in external help' (p.61) even if this meant admission to care. As one mother said, 'it's for control that they're in care'.

The implications for social workers about clients' views of appropriate use of authority are complex. The worker needs to be aware of different approaches to the use of authority and control by clients: where the client's expectation is of power-sharing worker control will be resented, but where the client's expectation is of worker-control an attempt at a more mutual approach may be seen as ineffectual. Even where a client does expect some form of authority they 'do not wish social workers to impose this on them in an arbitrary manner' (Rees and Wallace, 1982). Sainsbury (1975) found that clients who appreciated firmness and authority also valued 'understanding', 'honesty' and an empathic response from the worker. Finally while clients may wish workers to take control, the social worker cannot necessarily take over all responsibility for the client's problems and may validly have other concerns about promoting dependency and disempowering clients.

The issue of responsibility is likely to be perceived differently by client and worker. For example, Fisher *et al.* (1986) suggest that where parents were having difficulties in exercising care and control over their children 'they were looking to transfer the responsibility they felt to someone who would exercise the authority they felt their child lacked', whereas the workers were indeed attempting to involve parents actively in the solving the problems.

These differing perceptions suggest a 'clash in perspective' between worker and client. In a study of clients of the Family Welfare Association, Mayer and Timms (1970) found that clients who felt they needed *material* help perceived the social worker as offering *relationship* help instead. Clients who went for help with *emotional* problems wanted something done about *another* person (spouse, child) whereas the social worker tended to focus on the client. As Davies (1985) points out 'So numerous are such examples in the literature that one might be forgiven for thinking that what have been called "pervasive disagreements" are an inherent part of the social work process' (p.22).

Maluccio (1979) found that lack of agreement between worker and client about the nature of the problem was one of the most important factors associated with a poor outcome. In examining children's entry to residential care Fisher *et al.* (1986) identified a 'fundamental discrepancy' in approach between parents and workers. In general social workers 'took as a fundamental tenet that the genesis of child-care problems lies in family relationships' and, therefore, 'sought solutions in "talking things through"' (p.48). If this approach failed to solve the problem, the workers attributed this to the parents' active unwillingness to see themselves as part of the problem. Other explanations about parents' behaviour were not explored. Parents' feelings of being out of control and therefore resigned to the inevitability of social workers taking action were interpreted as lack of interest or coldness.

In one small-scale study agreement about purpose emerged as an important factor affecting outcome (Lishman, 1985). If clients and social workers did not share a contract and sense of purpose, then, however understanding or positive the social worker was, the client felt that nothing was achieved. This lack of a shared purpose is conveyed in the following perceptions.

Client: 'I didn't know what he was after, he wouldn't say. I thought he would try and find some way of it being my fault.'
Worker: 'He came for advice and management of the children but that's not what we tend to do. He is very strict and controlling – the children's problems may be a response to this.'

It seems obvious that the interests and purpose of clients and social workers will not always coincide. The lesson from client studies, however, is not that social workers and their clients can always agree totally, but that social workers have the responsibility for clarifying expectations and checking out how much they are agreed. Even where they differ, honest acknowledgement of the differences is a better base for work than discrepant assumptions on both sides which are never checked or challenged.

If agreement about purpose is established, the act of unburdening and the worker's ability to listen, to be empathic and to be non-judgemental may be effective from the client's point of view. Particularly if clients are experiencing interpersonal or mental health problems such an unburdening may be a relief. As one client (Lishman, 1985) expressed it 'I got a lot off my chest – it had been inside for a long time.'

How effective is such unburdening in the long term? For it to be effective it must lead to something: material help, advice and guidance or insight.

Families with multiple problems stressed the importance of material or financial help. Fathers in George and Wilding's (1972) study of motherless families were particularly critical when the social services failed to provide resources such as home helps and day-care facilities.

Parents of children with learning difficulties valued the opportunity to unburden. 'It's given me a chance to talk, otherwise it would have built up inside me having a child like *K*' (Glampson and Goldberg, 1976).

They felt they did not get enough such support, at the time of diagnosis, and during the period until the child entered school (Bedfordshire Social Services Department, 1978). However they were most critical of the lack of practical information and support.

People who were physically disabled stressed the importance of practical help such as aids and adaptations. They valued practical help which was regular and reliable such as home helps. They were particularly critical when, instead of negotiating such practical help, the social worker offered casework 'coming to terms with it' or 'just talked' (Blaxter, 1976).

Probationers and prisoners appear to have relatively clear expectations of social work: for prisoners, practical help in relation to housing, material resources, and children's behaviour: for probationers, practical help with employment, school or finance (Sainsbury and Nixon, 1979; Gandy *et al.*, 1975). Probationers and their families also valued an advocacy or negotiating role.

As we have already seen, clients are likely to perceive direct advice and guidance as more effective than a passive approach, and this was particularly true if they had interpersonal problems, e.g. about a child-care problem. Unburdening could sometimes be effective if it led to insight rather than to advice, e.g. one client said 'I realised, I was too possessive with my daughter', and another 'I found I was channelling anger from my husband onto my son and using my daughter as a buffer' (Lishman, 1985). However these insights were only effective because they led to changed behaviour and relationship patterns.

In conclusion, what lessons for social work practice do the client studies contain?

First, in order for it to be possible to engage with a client, the worker needs to show warmth, empathy, active listening and a non-judgemental approach. However these qualities are not enough for effective work. For this the worker needs to have relevant experience and show appropriate knowledge. Many clients wished the worker to be directive and exercise firm, if benevolent, authority over them. Advice, guidance, advocacy and activity on the part of the worker are seen by clients as essential for effective work. Finally it is necessary for the worker to take responsibility for clarifying expectations and assumptions about the purpose of contact. Lack of agreement about purpose is a major factor contributing to poor outcomes of contact.

3

Kinds of Communication

As we have seen, our clients evaluate and interpret our communications, both positively and negatively:

'Well, she's 'omely. She doesn't talk posh so you can talk to her properly' (Cohen, 1971)

'She's easy to talk to. I just relaxed. She has a calming effect' (Lishman, 1985)

Such apparently simple judgements are likely to reflect a social worker's use of a complex interaction of verbal, non-verbal and symbolic communications. This chapter introduces and defines these three kinds of interpersonal communication: symbolic, non-verbal and verbal.

Symbolic communication

According to the Shorter Oxford English Dictionary symbolic means 'expressed, denoted or conveyed by a symbol'. Symbolic communication, therefore, involves behaviour, actions or communications which represent or denote something else. As social workers we need to be aware of the potential meaning of our presentation, actions and aspects of our work environment. For example, our punctuality, our dress, the layout of our rooms, the food we provide for clients and the physical care we give them will have a symbolic, as well as literal, meaning for our clients.

Davis (1989) stresses the importance in residential care of the five senses; smell, touch and taste have particular relevance to symbolic communication. For example, stale cooking smells, fresh baking smells, the smell of incontinence, rough physical handling, a gentle hug, appetising, familiar food again all have a symbolic as well as literal and

practical meaning to residents. Such details of our practice may symbolise love, respect, care, control, power and other significant aspects of
our client–worker relationships.

The symbolism of the physical environment is of particular importance in residential care, since this is the daily living space of residents,
not just a venue of weekly contact. Davis (1989) comments 'the environments we provide speak directly to residents. Frankly some institu-
tions I have visited in the last couple of years have said quite plainly to
them "This is good enough for you".'

Basic care may be carried out in a variety ways each of which convey a
symbolic meaning. It may be done roughly and with haste, routinely,
functionally and efficiently, or (a different message) with time, sensitivity
and individualised care. Take, for example, group care for adolescent girls
with severe learning difficulties. Bathing with bubble bath, or gentle hair
washing, drying and brushing symbolise respect and value for the girls'
bodies and their physical care and appearance. Davis (1989) makes a similar point about the symbolic communication involved in the way a
worker treats the treasured possessions of a child in care. 'Caring for his
and her belongings is another way of caring for the child' (p.256).

Food and its presentation are highly symbolic. A residential worker
expressed surprise at the way the children in his care became quite
aggressive and disturbed when the milk ran out. They understood that
food (and especially milk) is a symbol of basic love and care. If we are
dealing with children in care who have been physically and emotionally
deprived, the importance of an abundance of food they enjoy cannot be
overemphasised. For them love must not run out. Poor quality of food or
inadequate quantity conveys a lack of care for any resident. How much
individual preferences are taken into account symbolises how much
attention and sensitivity is paid to cultural preferences and requirements
in food. An assessment centre whose residents are predominantly West
Indian and which routinely serves a white, British diet of fish and chips
and mince makes a symbolic statement about ethnicity and power.

In fieldwork a client's first contact with the service is usually the
receptionist and the waiting area. Hall (1974) found that clients were
often treated unsympathetically and insensitively by receptionists. My
experiences of reception (while visiting students on placement) vary. A
quick reception, a warm smile and the offer of a seat convey respect,
concern and that I am welcome. In contrast, being ignored for fifteen
minutes while a receptionist dealt with the telephone engineer and
numerous phone calls not only left me feeling enraged but also

conveyed a lack of respect and acknowledgement of myself as a person. For clients who already experience a sense of shame and stigma being ignored or rudely or abruptly treated symbolises a devaluing lack of respect and confirmation of lack of worth.

Waiting areas vary. Space, comfortable seating, cleanliness, fresh paint, a variety of comics, toys and magazines convey a welcome. Peeling walls, dirt, a smell of urine, and broken furniture convey symbolically that the waiting client is worth no more than this. Oliver's survey (1990) of a small selection of social service reception areas presents a depressing picture of reception and waiting areas, with few public toilets, poor access for wheel-chairs, reception hatches high in the walls, unaccessible to wheel-chairs and creating a barrier to communication, and few toys for children. While the threat of violence has influenced departments' reception areas, so that some 'adopt a siege mentality', Oliver supports Kent Social Services Department's view that respect for the client, conveyed by pleasant surroundings and service, may go some way to prevent anger arising, although staff should also be protected, e.g. by buzzers and closed circuit television.

Similarly, interviewing rooms which are cramped, used as second-hand clothing stores, inadequately soundproofed and uncomfortably furnished symbolically devalue the client, the worker and the interview process.

Breakwell and Rowett (1982) remind us that the interview room is the social worker's and not the client's territory. Clients entering a social worker's room are expected to respect territorial rules, e.g. not to move chairs, or sit on the desk. Breakwell and Rowett note how symbolic of power and control territory can be. In general clients respect our symbols of authority and legitimacy embedded in our territory, e.g. desk, forms and records, but we should be aware of our need for and use of these symbols and their meaning in terms of authority and control.

The way in which seats are arranged is symbolic of territory and power. If I sit behind my desk, formality is increased, distance (emotional as well as physical) maintained and my formal authority intensified. Without the protection of my desk I am less threatening, my power and authority less obtrusive, and physically my position lends itself to more equality. However placing a client in a lower chair than the social worker again puts the client in an inferior position and symbolises the power differential in the relationship.

D'Ardenne and Mahtani (1989) are also concerned with symbolic aspects of physical space or territory. In particular they argue that 'the physical environment can be a powerful statement of your transcultural viewpoint'(p.53). They suggest, for example, that pictures or photographs in an office will be 'more welcoming' to clients of different ethnic origins if they 'depict people from different cultures or show different parts of the world'. Similar considerations apply to the physical environment as a statement of class.

The way we dress communicates symbolically something of ourselves, and will have symbolic meaning for clients (and colleagues) depending on age, culture, class and context.

Dress may be particularly important in terms of first impressions. When we meet someone for the first time there is so much to take in that we have to be selective. Dress, hair and facial expression are immediately available to us, if we are sighted, and on the basis of them we tend to make assumptions about personality, character or behaviour. So, for example, untidy dress and appearance may be interpreted as signifying carelessness or incompetence.

A formal suit, male or female, may convey distance and power, not necessarily appropriate to a fieldwork interview, and certainly inappropriate in everyday life in residential work. In a multidisciplinary setting, where people from more powerful disciplines, e.g. medicine, besuit themselves, the formal suit may represent the social worker's claim to equivalent authority. It may also be accepted by clients as the uniform of the place.

In a court setting, failure by a male worker to wear a suit and tie, or by a female worker to wear a skirt may be seen by magistrate, sheriff or judge as implying a lack of respect for judicial processes, or a lack of power or authority on the part of the social worker. Such assumptions, based on appearance, can be detrimental to clients.

What messages may be conveyed by a young social worker's choice of a mini skirt? For her it is comfortable, fashionable and attractive. For the Muslim father of the family she is visiting it may flaunt sexuality and symbolise an attack on his cultural values and his relations with women, in particular his wife. The same mini-skirt in a hospital ward round may equally symbolise sexuality, youth and a lack of authority, in some sense diminishing the female social worker's role and contribution in relation to the power of the male medical hierarchy.

Punctuality, reliability, and attention to detail can be symbolic of the worker's care, concern and competence. A couple applied to adopt a child. At the first interview the social worker arrived two hours late and then took down information on the inside of a cigarette packet. The couple, who were anxious at the prospect of assessment, experienced the lateness as insensitive, offhand and unconcerned. The cigarette packet symbolised lack of thought and preparation.

Unreliability ('he never does what he promises') symbolises for many clients a lack of 'genuine concern' (Rees and Wallace, 1982). It may also remind them or reawaken feelings about unreliability of significant people. For example, for many children in care, parents or attachment figures will have been 'unreliable' in major ways, e.g. by illness, separation or rejection. Bowlby (1984) suggest 'whatever representational models of attachment figures and of self an individual builds during his childhood and adolescence, tend to persist relatively unchanged into and throughout adult life' (p.141). We need, as social workers, to be aware that our own lack of reliability, even in relatively minor ways, such as forgetting, not only symbolises a current lack of concern, but may confirm and strengthen earlier attachment models of unreliable care.

In Chapter 2 we saw that activity on the part of the social worker was seen by clients as symbolising concern; the following comments from clients (Sainbury *et al.*,1982, p.76) illustrate satisfaction and dissatisfaction on this theme:

'He really gets down to my problems. If I had to change (my social worker) my only worry would be, would he take an active part in helping us?'

'He says "I'll see what I can do", but you never hear he's done it.'

While social workers' use of activity as a means of conveying concern has to be balanced against the danger of 'taking over', and disempowering clients, if we promise action and fail to carry it out we will inevitably convey a lack of concern.

If we recognise the importance of the symbolic meaning of our behaviour, dress and environment, we can use this to enhance our clients' feelings of self-worth and of our concern, reliability and competence.

Non-verbal communication

As with symbolic communication social workers need to be aware of the potential meaning to others of their non-verbal behaviour including facial expression, gaze, orientation and body movement.

Sutton (1979) suggests that while spoken communication is concerned mainly with information-giving, non-verbal communication is 'the music behind the words' conveying feelings or attitudes.

How important is non-verbal communication? Argyle *et al.* (1970) found that, in relation to behaviour conveying dominance or submission, non-verbal communication had more effect than verbal, and that if the two were in conflict the verbal communication tended to be ignored.

While non-verbal communication is important, it is also difficult to interpret. For example, nodding one's head is not a single activity; it can act as a reinforcer (when one person's behaviour is followed by a head nod from the other the behaviour increases) or give the other person permission to go on speaking. It can be the sign of attentive listening, but a series of rapid head nods can convey that the nodder wishes to speak (Argyle, 1975).

We need to be aware of the ambiguity of non-verbal communication (e.g. a swinging foot can convey anger, fear, boredom or energy) and of the context (e.g. the person's normal non-verbal style). Nicolson and Bayne (1984) suggest that it is changes in non-verbal behaviour or untypical behaviour which are particularly significant, e.g. avoiding eye contact or fidgeting more when discussing a particular issue.

Since interactions between social workers and clients may involve mutual difficulties in interpreting such ambiguous non-verbal behaviour, it is essential that the social worker is aware of her or his non-verbal style and of how congruent her or his verbal and non-verbal communications are. Feedback from video is the most direct way to see ourselves and our non-verbal communication as others see us. While the awareness given may initially lead to self-consciousness and feelings of being deskilled the potential for changing behaviour, of which we were previously unaware, is clear.

The context of our work will affect the significance of our non-verbal communication. Children seem particularly aware of and sensitive to non-verbal behaviour. In working with deaf people our posture, position and facial expression will be particularly important; with blind people our voice, tone and touch. In residential work our non-verbal behaviour is constantly on view.

Non-verbal communication can be broadly divided into two areas: proxemics concerned with distance and how close people like to be to each other and kinesics referring to movements, gestures, expression and eye contact. More simply we can consider the following areas: distance, posture and orientation, gaze and eye contact, and facial expression.

We have already considered the symbolic aspects of territory and space. We must also be aware of what interpersonal distance or closeness is comfortable to ourselves and our clients. Preferences for closeness or distance are affected by race, gender, class, individual, and by whom we are with, how well we know them and how we feel about them. There are marked cross-cultural differences in how close people like to be to each other: e.g. Swedes and Scots are most distant (Lott *et al.*, 1969). Women tend to tolerate greater physical closeness (Mehrabian, 1972). There are no fixed rules for distance: getting too close can seem intrusive and threatening, remaining too distant can seem cold and withdrawn.

Proximity also needs to be considered in relation to orientation. Sommer (1965) and Cook (1968) explored different seating positions and found evidence which suggested that sitting alongside a person implies cooperation, opposite a person competition and at right angles to each equality of status. Thus sitting behind a desk, directly opposite a client, has distancing and power implications but also may be confrontational.

Posture is also important, reflecting cultural and contextual conventions (sitting up straight in church), status and emotions, For example, Mehrabian (1972) found that subjects were more likely to be relaxed with a low status person: such 'relaxation' involved reclining, leaning sidewards and placing arms and legs asymmetrically. As social workers we may need to consider whether our relaxed posture (intended to make our clients feel comfortable) may denote our assumption of power and status.

Posture can convey attitudes. Mehrabian (1972) found that we convey a positive attitude by reasonably relaxed open posture with uncrossed limbs, and by turning towards and slightly leaning towards our clients. Such a posture helps to convey our warmth and immediacy, openness to the client and attentiveness. However there are no fixed rules about posture: being too relaxed may convey power and inattentiveness, being too rigid, tension, anxiety and authority.

Touch is another aspect of proxemics which may vary in meaning according to context and client. Like distance there are cultural differences in the use of touch. For example, Argyle (1973, p.86) notes that 'in parts of Africa and Asia it is normal for two interactors to be in bodily contact'. In contrast, in the North of Scotland, except in intimate relationships, touch is likely to be viewed as intrusion into personal space. In social work, individual and contextual differences also matter. In working with people who are bereaved touch seems an important means of conveying concern and openness to the bereaved person's distress. A pat or brief hug can convey encouragement and support. Sometimes, however, it may be done to protect ourselves, e.g. hugging to 'comfort' and thereby stop a client's extreme distress also protects us from having to share it. Touch may be interpreted sexually: for example, for a child or woman who has been sexually abused, touch may symbolise and reawaken the abuse of power and violation of boundaries. Sadly, anxieties about sexuality in residential child-care may lead to a taboo on touch at the expense of touch as a 'rewarding and undervalued way of making contact with inarticulate, distressed or emotionally isolated children and adolescents' (Davis, 1989, p.257).

Kinesics includes the use of eye contact, facial expression, movements and gestures. Eye contact or gaze appears to have an important function in regulating conversation. For example, in a conversation one participant looks at the other more when he or she is listening than when speaking. A participant looks at the other when she/he finishes speaking, and away at the beginning of speaking, thus signalling the beginning and end of her/his utterances (Kendon, 1973). So, when a client is speaking we need to keep looking at him or her, thus conveying our attention.

Eye contact can convey liking or positive attitudes, but prolonged eye contact can also signify interest in the other person, either in a friendly, sexual or aggressive way (Argyle, 1973). Eye contact therefore, has to be used with discretion.

Eye contact differs according to culture and gender. Exline (1963) found that women engage in greater eye contact than men. Furnham and Bochner (1986) identify cultural differences in normal eye contact: Arab and Latin-American people have higher levels of mutual gaze than European people.

The level of appropriate eye contact cannot be specified. It has to be adjusted by the worker according to a client's cultural expectations. In general too much eye contact can be seen as staring and obtrusive. For a female social worker to engage in moderate eye contact with an Asian man may be seen as immodest, brazen and unsuitable. On the other hand too little eye contact can be seen as 'shifty' or convey embarrassment, fear or shyness. It can also represent deep thought and withdrawal into one's inner world, or suggest respect for the other's privacy.

Facial expressions are interpreted as conveying attitudes. For example, frowning may convey criticism: a bored expression may be perceived as disinterested or devaluing. Across all cultures smiling appears to convey a non-threatening approach and a positive and friendly attitude, although it does not necessarily denote happiness (Argyle,

1978). It may conceal anxiety, reflect a desire to please or represent social politeness. Smiling also appears to act as a social reinforcer. Greenspoon (1955) found that smiling, nodding one's head and leaning forward acted as reinforcers of the other person's behaviour, including the amount of speech and speech on selected topics. As social workers we need to be aware of such subliminal reinforcement and to use it discriminatingly. A worker who was anxious to engage with a rather withdrawn, inarticulate client, found herself continuing to smile as he disclosed more and more of his anti-social behaviour until she realised she was unwittingly conveying her approval of it.

Facial expression appears related to responsiveness. An immobile, unchanging facial expression can appear bland or withdrawn or unresponsive to another person's disclosure. Responsiveness also appears to be conveyed by body movement such as nodding one's head, gesticulating, moving one's arms and feet and leaning forward (Mehrabian and Williams, 1969). Again it is difficult to make rules. While lack of such activity conveys a lack of responsiveness, excessive activity and movement e.g. fiddling, rubbing oneself and frequently shifting position, can be distracting and convey a lack of attention (Reith, 1975). In a study of interviewing behaviour (Lishman, 1985) the level of non-verbal activity by social workers was higher than anticipated and did not appear distracting to clients. The one social worker who engaged in minimal bodily movement appeared rigid, immobile and rather unresponsive. The concept of 'non-verbal leakage', that our true feelings may leak out in non-verbal behaviour (Ekman and Friesen, 1968), appeared relevant to this worker in that his only movement was of his feet: it is possible that they conveyed what the rest of his consciously controlled non-verbal behaviour concealed, e.g. anxiety or irritation.

Finally, Henly's (1979) reminder about the role of non-verbal feedback in relation to transcultural communication is potentially relevant to all our communication with our clients. Non-verbal communication from clients can inform us how much they feel comfortable with us and how much is being understood, e.g. a glazed expression, a fixed smile and frequent shifts of position are likely to convey discomfort, with the relationship, with a communication, or with the purpose or structure of the interaction.

Symbolic and non-verbal behaviour represent powerful aspects of our communication. They convey messages about class, culture, ethnicity and gender, power, control and authority, and about genuineness, concern, respect and caring. It is our responsibility to continue to increase our awareness of our own communications, by feedback from clients, colleagues, role play and video, and to monitor and check out our interpretations of clients' symbolic and non-verbal communication.

Verbal communication

Verbal communication means oral or spoken communication. Verbal communication in social work can be considered either in terms of its purposes or of the skills involved.

Here I examine briefly the *skills* involved in verbal communication. Subsequent chapters examine them more fully in relation to different purposes of social work and apply them more fully to practice.

Questioning or probing

We tend to think of all exploration in terms of asking questions. Students, beginning to practise interviewing skills, often have the experience of falling into a question-and-answer routine in which the student feels more and more like an interrogator. Underlying this question-and-answer pattern can be an unstated assumption that the worker is the expert, the client has a problem which requires a solution and that once he/she has provided the information about this problem the worker/expert will provide the solution. How can we avoid this kind of unhelpful emphasis on question and answer?

First, we have to be aware whenever we *are* asking a question. Second, we have to think about the purpose of this question. Is the information it solicits essential? Does it help the client to tell his/her story? Third, is there an alternative to asking this question? Would paraphrasing what the client has said, or reflecting back his/her underlying feeling, more usefully explore the client's preoccupation or problem? Finally, if asking a question seems appropriate and essential, what types of questions might we ask?

Closed and open questions   *Closed* questions tend to invite a yes/no answer, or a small number of possible responses, e.g.

'Are you employed/married?' tends to invite a 'yes' or 'no' reply.

'How many children do you have?', while not inviting a simple yes/no answer, will tend to be answered in a limited way.

Open questions invite a wider range of responses and the interviewee is free to choose how to respond, e.g.

'And what about your children?'

'What did you think when he said that?'

Such questions invite the respondent to share their views, feelings or opinions.

Closed questions used too frequently tend to develop into a question-and-answer routine, but can be useful foɪ gaining specific information. Open questions help clients to tell their story better or explore their problem or situation.

Direct and indirect questions   *Direct* questions are straight questions or queries, e.g. 'How did you manage on Social Security?'

Indirect questions imply a question but indirectly without a question mark at the end, e.g. 'It must be hard managing on Social Security.'

By making a question indirect we can make it more open and leave the client greater choice about how to respond.

Probing   Egan (1986, p.111) defines prompts and probes as 'verbal tactics for helping clients talk about themselves and define their problems more concretely and specifically'. Probes can be open or indirect questions or requests to help clients talk about their concerns:

'You sound very upset, but I'm not quite sure what it's about.'

'You said that you and Jane have had several rows this week. Perhaps you could tell me a bit more what they are about.'

A probe can also be an 'accent', a one- or two-word restatement highlighting a client's previous response:

'I was a bit annoyed with her at the time.'

'A *bit* annoyed?'

'Well, actually, I was furious.'

Reflection

Reflection involves showing our clients that we understand their feelings and experience by reflecting or feeding back to them what they have conveyed to us.

Reflecting may simply involve picking up a word or phrase a client has used and feeding it back, implying a request to hear more, e.g.

'You felt relieved...?'

Reflecting in this way involves selection, and it is important to select on the basis of what seems important to the client, rather than of interest to the worker.

Reflecting can take the form of paraphrasing: rephrasing or repeating what the client has said in different words. It is difficult to do this accurately: to find a way of saying what the other has said, using different words, but conveying exactly the same meaning. Paraphrasing can be cognitive, about understanding or content, 'You mean that ...?' It can also be affective, reflecting back feelings. Again this is difficult, it involves interpreting not just what the client has said, but his/her tone, facial expression and body movement. Some emotions may be seen as general – 'You feel angry ...? sad? helpless? anxious?' but some are much more specific, e.g. 'humiliated', 'vindicated', 'cheated'.

Paraphrasing to a client needs to be done tentatively: it is a means of checking out whether the worker is correctly understanding how the client feels or sees things. It indicates that the worker is attending to the client, and, by checking out, it facilitates further exploration.

Conveying empathy

Conveying empathy goes beyond reflection: not only does the worker convey understanding of the client's feelings but also a willingness to enter into them or show them. Egan (1986, p.95) defines empathy as 'the ability to *enter into* and understand the world of another person and to communicate this understanding to him or her'. He suggests that responding empathically involves asking 'What is the core message being expressed at this point?' For him the technology of conveying basic empathy involves both identifying and reflecting back the client's feelings 'you feel...' with accurate emotion and an identification of the experiences or behaviours underlying these feelings, 'you feel... because?', e.g:

'You *feel* so angry *because* it's as if your father is abusing you again?'

Accurate empathic responses such as this can help a client to explore further problematic areas or feelings, and identify and focus on key issues and feelings.

We need to take time to think about the client's core message and not rush in with an attempted empathic response. Our responses need to be brief or they interfere with the client's story or self exploration. Empathy is not conveyed by the following responses:

- no response – the client may feel the issue or feeling is not worthy of a response, or simply not understood;
- a question – again, this deflects from or ignores the core message;
- a cliché – this trivialises the uniqueness and significance of this particular client;
- immediate action – this deflects from and ignores the client's feelings.

Focusing

Focusing, in a non-optical sense, means concentrating on. Within an interview exploration of a client's situation can be wide-ranging, sometimes apparently tangential, and the worker struggles to hold on to a focus, or a purpose, for the interview. The worker has to balance potentially conflicting themes:

- the need to keep the focus broad enough not to miss or ignore relevant material;
- the need to focus on some of the content at greater emotional depth;
- the need to focus discussion and guide it towards a goal.

Focusing, in this sense, links with Egan's 'finding the core message'. i.e. what is the client really concerned about and can I help him/her to focus on that? Sometimes what a client is concerned about may be what is *not* said, e.g. anxiety about illness or death often seems too frightening to raise, and what is talked about is almost a smoke-screen.

Clients often come to a social worker with multiple and complex problems, e.g. debt, mental health problems and difficulties with the children. These can be overwhelming for client and worker if some more limited focus is not agreed on. Where can we start?

Egan (1986) suggests a set of principles which may help the worker to focus:

- If the client is in a crisis, start with the crisis.
- Focus on what the client sees as important or feels as most painful.
- Focus on an issue the client is ready to work on even if it does not seem the most important one to the worker.
- Focus on a sub-problem which is manageable and relatively amenable to success. This gives the client a sense of success and empowerment which may have a knock-on effect on other problems. For example, paying off the electricity bill may aid more patient and consistent parenting.

Summarising

Summarising is a means of clarifying what the client has been saying and an aid to focusing. In a sense it is like an extended paraphrase. We listen to what the client has said, select what seem the key issues and feed back in shortened form and different words but trying to convey the essence of what the client has been saying. Again, our aim is to check that the worker's understanding of content and feeling corresponds with the client's. Again a danger is that in selecting for the summary, the worker may omit an issue of importance to the client.

Egan (1986) points out that, properly done, summarising can help clients clarify issues within their own perspective, and help them to develop different or alternative perspectives. 'Often when scattered elements are brought together, the client sees the "bigger picture" more clearly' (p.173). Egan suggests summaries can be particularly helpful at certain times:

- At the beginning of a new session: the client cannot then start where he/she was before but must move on.

- When a session is going nowhere: summarising can stop rambling and allow worker and client to ask 'Where do we go from here?'
- When a client gets stuck: again a summary may help the client see a new perspective and thereby move on.

Confrontation and challenging

Chambers English Dictionary (1988) defines confrontation as 'continued hostile attitude, with hostile acts but without declaration of war' and it is in this sense that confrontation in social work is often feared, because of connotations of aggression, destructiveness and personal attack. 'When confrontation is actually an attack, it serves the purpose of helping the confronter to get a load off his or her chest rather than helping the other person live more effectively' (Egan, 1986, p.219).

In contrast Carkhuff (1969) views confrontation as a useful skill, 'whereby the helper conveys his or her understanding of discrepancies in the client's behaviour, feelings or thinking. These discrepancies can be between:

- The clients' views of how they would like to be and how they think they actually are.
- How clients say they feel and how they actually behave.
- How clients say they feel and behave and how the worker experiences them.'

Carkhuff (1969) and Fischer (1978) argue that a worker who is empathic will also be aware of discrepancies like these. However, any confrontation about these discrepancies needs to be for the clients' understanding and change and not the worker's relief or ventilation. It should focus on client strengths rather than weaknesses.

Nelson-Jones (1983) uses the term 'challenging' to mean 'reflecting and/or focusing on discrepancies in thoughts, feelings and actions. The *how* of confrontations or challenges is just as important as their *what* or verbal content' (p.111). Egan (1986) suggests that challenging is more than confronting. It involves helping clients 'understand themselves, others and the world more fully and constructively'. Challenging in Egan's sense helps the client to gain a new perspective. While challenging discrepancies is one way of doing this, giving new information or correcting misinformation can be another. For example, a client who had been suddenly bereaved expressed the anxiety that she was 'going mad'. She was greatly relieved to hear a radio programme about grief, where it was made clear that many bereaved people similarly felt they were going mad. As a result of this new information her anxiety about it was considerably lessened.

Hindrances to communication

What conditions may hinder or block communication between a worker and client?

Environment   The physical environment can impede communication, e.g. a hot stuffy room can lessen concentration. Television can be a distraction in a home visit: nevertheless the worker has to assess 'whether and when it is helpful to ask that it be turned off' and to remember that if we make such a request, this conveys the message 'I am the one who is defining this situation' (Sutton, 1979).

Interruptions   Interruptions, e.g. telephone calls, a knock at the door, are distracting and interrupt the flow of communication.

Overload   There are limits to the amount of information a person can take in when it is presented verbally. Complicated information, e.g. about entitlement to benefits, may be best given briefly verbally, and then reinforced by written information, to be digested over time.

Unchecked assumptions   Unspoken, and unchecked assumptions create misunderstanding. The 'clash in perspective' identified by Mayer and Timms (1970) is a major example of unchecked assumptions, e.g. when clients felt they needed material help, they perceived the workers as interested only in offering help with relationships.

Preoccupation   Anxiety or preoccupation with inner thoughts may limit our capacity to hear what the other person is saying, e.g. a child or old person about to be admitted to care, may fail to hear introductions because of high levels of anxiety.

Stereotyping   Stereotyping can distort communications. A stereotype is a 'fixed, conventionalised representation', e.g. the stereotype of a social worker as long-haired, left-wing and *Guardian*-reading. Stereotyping involves a process of assigning people to categories on the basis of nationality, race, class, occupation, age or appearance and then inferring general characteristics on the basis of the category.

Stereotyping can be useful in social relationships: 'Social intercourse would become chaotic if we did not straightaway react differently to a sixty-year-old and a six-year-old, to a society hostess and a prostitute' (Vernon, 1964, in Cook, 1968, p.4). However stereotyping becomes a communication block if rigidly applied and unchecked. A client may be unable to hear what a worker says if he or she has stereotyped the worker as too young and casual (on the basis of wearing jeans), too middle-aged and middle-class, or a man ('all men are brutes').

Experience Past experience can impede communication whether the experience is conscious and remembered, or unconscious. A client whose previous experience of social work was offhand or dismissive or who had been judged 'unworthy' of help (Rees, 1974, 1978) is likely to be more sensitive to perceived slights or rejection in a new social work encounter.

Transference, the unconscious transfer of feelings from a client's past onto the worker, can also distort communication. For example, if a client has been consistently criticised and rejected in childhood by her parents she may unconsciously expect the worker to be similarly critical and rejecting, she may interpret positive or neutral aspects of the workers' communication as critical, and she may also even appear to elicit such criticism and rejection.

If the worker is able to see the distorted perception and communication in terms of transference (and understand where in the client's past it comes from) at the least it may enable the worker to manage the client's negative communication, or at best enable the worker to explore with the client the feelings from the past and disentangle how they distort current communication and relationships.

Translation A final but crucial block to verbal communication is in the use of language. Client and worker may not share a common language and an interpreter may be required. While a family member, friend or neighbour may be willing there are potential dangers in using an unofficial interpreter. Shackman (1985) lists some including:

- inaccurate translation, bias or distortion;

- lack of confidentiality;
- failure of the unofficial interpreter to understand the role of interpreter.

A family member may have a particular view about a client's problem and wish to promote it. He or she may over-identify with the client or worker. Using the client's children is particularly difficult, if the discussion is of sensitive, painful issues or areas not seen by the client as appropriate for the child to be involved in.

For example, a male social worker was asked to see a Bangladeshi woman who was confined to her flat and appeared to be depressed. The social worker invited her teenage daughter to interpret. Although the daughter was bilingual and appeared to understand the social worker her mother said almost nothing. Only a change of worker and of interpreter moved communication forward. The male social worker was replaced by a female, the child by a formal, non-related female interpreter. It then emerged that the mother has been suffering from gynaecological problems which she could not discuss with her male GP. She then felt it completely inappropriate to share such intimate details with either her daughter or male social worker. Thus, gender, race, generational boundaries and language all acted as blocks to open communication.

If an official interpreter is necessary and is available, what factors should be considered? Shackman (1985) provides the following advice:

- Check that the interpreter and client do speak the same language or dialect.
- Use clear, simple language.
- Clarify with the interpreter the purpose and focus of the interview and ensure that he or she understands the need for a comprehensive and fairly literal translation.
- Listen to both the interpreter and client, engage in eye contact with both and note their non-verbal behaviour.
- Check regularly with the interpreter that the client understands the dialogue.
- Take time at the end to review the interview with the interpreter.

Working with an interpreter, therefore, requires additional communication skills including clarity and simplicity of language and sensitivity to non-verbal communication. It also requires time, concentration, patience and a readiness to slow down the pace of the interview.

Even if client and worker speak English they may not share the same verbal form. D'Ardenne and Mahtani (1989) point out that 'English-speaking counsellors expect their clients to share their manner of speech. When they do not, counsellors may devalue their clients, either by believing they are intellectually slow or that they are uneducated' (p.64). They argue that 'black clients who speak another form of English, for example, are even less likely to be understood by their counsellors than those who speak another language and require inter-preters' (p.64). However, working-class white people can also experi-ence such language disadvantage and discrimination.

If undue emphasis is placed on verbal communication, clients who are less articulate or lack complex verbal skills, including some people with learning difficulties, or children and adolescents will be disadvantaged.

Written reports

While social workers frequently use different kinds of written communication, e.g. letters, records and reports, discussion of written communication skills in social work literature tends to be neglected, although Bottoms and Stelman (1988) provide more specific and detailed guidance about Social Inquiry Reports. This chapter also runs the risk of failing to do justice to the complexity of written commun-ication skills required in social work. Only general guidelines can be given, and, as with verbal communication skills, while a written analysis may provide useful pointers, skills are learned in action, with practice and feedback.

Hargie (1986) acknowledges criticism that social work records and reports are often 'lengthy, rambling and anecdotal' and suggests 'writ-ten reports should be clear, concise and concentrate' on the important features of the case. This is sensible to prescribe but more difficult to carry out. Brevity is important; a long, dense block of text is offputting to the reader. Social work reports, in common with other reports, need short paragraphs and sub-headings to break up the text and key the reader into the main points.

If we take a Social Inquiry Report (in Scotland these are undertaken by local authority social workers) as an example, the considerations involved in preparing and presenting such a report are also relevant to other formal reports.

First we need to consider the *purpose* of a report since that will define not only the content but also the structure and presentation. In Scotland a Social Inquiry Report is compiled 'with a view to assisting the Court in determining the most suitable method of dealing with any person in respect of an offence' (Criminal Justice (Scotland) Act, 1949). Thus the Social Inquiry Report is intended as a means of providing information to the Court to assist it to deal with the accused. However the report is also shown to the accused and must be understandable by him or her.

What qualities of the report will best achieve this purpose? It needs to be written in clear, straightforward language. It should avoid professional jargon. Use of such phrases as 'structural factors', 'deviant sub-culture', 'material deprivation' alienate the non-social-worker reader. The report must contain *accurate* information, carefully checked and scrutinised. It must distinguish between evidence and opinion.

At the beginning the report needs identifying details, including age, religion, marital status, and details of the offence. Thereafter the writer has to balance the relative advantages of using a consistent structure for all reports, and the need to individualise each report. Consistency of headings across reports helps the Court to familiarise itself quickly with the contents of an individual report, but a stereotyped presentation will fail to present important information early and thereby highlight it. For example, a recent family death, conflict with a step-parent, or changes in drinking patterns, presented late on in a report in accordance with the standard format will fail to highlight the significance of such factors. Such a failure fails in the purpose of the report: to give the Court the necessary information to deal with the accused.

The report-writer therefore needs to combine a broad, consistent structure with a need to be flexible according to the requirements of presenting information about this particular offender.

The structure of the report can be seen as having a narrowing focus beginning with the breadth of the subject's family life and relationships and narrowing to consideration of the particular offence. Headings could then be as follows:

- Family details and relationships.
- The offender in relation to his family.
- Work, finance.
- Associated, leisure, drink patterns.
- Personality assessment.
- Previous offending behaviour.

- Characteristics of present offence.
- Social work possibilities inherent in the court's decision, if applicable.

The Central Council for Education and Training in Social Work (CCETSW) (1992) draws a helpful distinction between information relevant to offending and information relevant to sentence or disposal. Information related to offending includes circumstances surrounding the offence, the subject's offending history and the subject's personal and social circumstances, including health, drug or alchohol misuse, family responsibilities, employment and housing.

Information relevant to sentencing or disposal includes previous court disposals, income and financial information, health, family responsibilities, employment and housing. CCETSW (1992) recommends that a Social Inquiry Report always contains 'a reference to the subject's physical and mental health, including whether or not the subject has problems associated with the use of alcohol or other drugs' (91.5).

Finally, the report has to be concluded. While the report must not appear to usurp the Court's function of deciding appropriate disposal it is now accepted that a report may contain a recommendation and the Streatfield Report (1961) argues that the expression of an 'opinion' was an integral part of the report. However the writer should not feel compelled to submit a view in every report. If he or she feels in doubt, e.g. because of inadequate knowledge of this offender or the likely consequences of a particular disposal, a recommendation should be left out. Any expression of opinion, like any conclusion, has to follow from the evidence in the report. A final paragraph, even without a recommendation, needs to identify and summarise key factors relevant to the Court's decision about disposal.

Similar considerations would apply to reports to the Children's Hearings in Scotland. Here a front sheet contains 'hard' basic information about child and family. The body of the report concentrates on areas not dissimilar to the Social Inquiry Report including:

- Family relationships – relationship between parents, parental roles and authority. Social habits of the parents, relationships between child and parents and between child and siblings.
- Criminality in the family.
- Finance.
- Leisure.
- School.

- Previous contacts with social work, the police or the Hearing.
- Personality.

The writer needs to use simple, clear language and avoid jargon since the Hearing members are lay people and the report is shared with the family. Again the writer has to balance the advantages of a common structure for reports with the need to present and highlight individual factors and issues relevant to this particular child. Again the social worker has to consider the purpose of the report: to provide an assessment which is a tool for the Hearing members to arrive at suitable ways of intervening on the child's behalf.

The report has to contain not just factual evidence but the worker's assessment of the reasons underlying this particular referral. For example, in stealing, investigation of group involvement, family poverty, family attitudes to crime, disposal of the goods or money, will provide clues to understanding patterns of behaviour, the needs of the child and therefore the most appropriate disposal.

The report requires a conclusion and again while it is for the Hearing to decide on how the referral is to be disposed, the social worker has to indicate the possible range of disposals meeting both the interests of the child, and the concerns of the public about safety and control.

Both these examples, Social Inquiry Reports and reports for the Hearings, illuminate skills and issues in report writing including clarity, simplicity, brevity, and the use of structure and flexibility.

Written records

Social workers spend a considerable amount of time engaged in recording, but like report-writing this is a neglected area in social work education and literature.

Before identifying the skills required to record clearly, accurately and appropriately it is necessary to examine the purpose of recording. Purposes are multiple and may be in conflict. Payne (1978) provides a framework to analyse the purpose of written records. However the analysis predates the legislation giving clients the right of access to files held on them by housing and social services departments. It examines the purpose of written records for the agency and the worker and is summarised here. Then the implications of client (as opposed to agency or worker) records are considered.

Agency records

Legal records   Some records are required by legislation to be kept by social service/work departments, e.g. the requirement to keep a register of blind people. Sometimes social workers themselves will choose to use their records as parts of legal proceedings, e.g. in child care. Sometimes, however, social work records may be subpoenaed by the court e.g. in access cases in divorce proceedings. Here accurate entries including dates and times of contact, are of paramount importance.

Similarly, in cases of abuse, records provide evidence which may be used in legal proceedings (both court proceedings concerned with the protection and welfare of a child and public inquiries investigating the practice of social workers and other professionals). Here again, accurate records of dates and times of contact (with parents, but particularly with the child) and detailed observation of his/her physical, cognitive, developmental and emotional development, current behaviour and current physical and emotional state are crucial.

Financial records   While information about clients' financial records may be kept separately from social work records, verification of clients' financial position may sometimes involve reference to social work records. There may be inherent conflict, e.g. checking parental contributions for children in residential care (with its implications of debt collection) involves a different purpose from the therapeutic intervention aimed at empowering and increasing coping strengths in a family.

Management control   Records can be used by management and workers to show that workers are complying with legal, agency or management requirements. Such records are used as part of hierarchical accountability procedures in senior management.

Accountability   Both recording and supervision involving verbal accounts of practice (Pithouse, 1987) are the main means by which social workers fulfil their accountability to management and to wider society. Davies (1985) argues that it was the Colwell inquiry (DHSS, 1974) which 'marked a watershed in pinpointing the accountability of social service departments in areas of public concern' (p.180).

The concept of accountability, applied to child care, child safety and child abuse has extended to other areas of social work practice so that as social workers, rightly, we have to account for decisions, assessments and work done. Perhaps the major concern about such accountability is if, in practice or recording, it leads us to a defensive, no-risk, 'covering ourselves' strategy, with, for example, a meticulous record of contact but an unwillingness in practice to consider any risk at all even where positive probabilities outweigh negative.

Information storage   An organisation may keep information for which there may be no immediate use but which has potential as a data bank of client need, agency resources and take-up of services. Reith (1988, p.31) argues that few information systems 'collect the kind of information about service processes and outcomes that would be useful to practitioners. Categories of client problems and agency responses tend to be crude, and the data elicited may not be very reliable'. However this is not inevitable. Freeman and Montgomery (1988) show how 'in-house' information systems in Strathclyde informed policy and practice in child care. For example, the Child Care Information System indicated that an increasing proportion of older children were coming into care from intact, two-parent families, because they were outwith parental control or relationships were deteriorating. One response was the setting-up of a short-stay refuge for such adolescents with the aim of preventing permanent breakdown and entry to care.

Agency evaluation   Information storage is closely linked with research and evaluation since agency records allow for a statistical analysis of work done. Particularly in voluntary organisations or short-term innovatory projects renewed funding is contingent upon a favourable evaluation. Such a requirement may threaten the traditional 'neutrality' of research. Finally, it may be difficult to separate such evaluation (complex as it is) from a political context.

For the practitioner many of the purposes for the agency of recording, outlined above, may seem rather remote. What are the purposes of records for the worker? How do they relate to agency recording?

Worker records

Record of work done   The record a social worker, or – in group care – a team, keeps 'covers' the individual or team and is the means by which they are accountable to their agency and even to society. For example, accurate records of visits made and of direct observations of children and the care they are receiving are essential evidence in child abuse work, but may also provide evidence and justification for worker action and decisions in a subsequent inquiry.

Supervision This is different from management control and accountability. Supervision is concerned with the personal development of effective work with clients. It is related to consultation and is a professional-to-professional relationship rather than a superior-to-subordinate one (Payne, 1978). Here records are a basis for extended discussion.

O'Hagan (1986) calls recording 'a crucial learning tool'. He argues that after a crisis, detailed scrutiny is essential 'although the temptation to walk away ... is difficult to resist.' Such recording facilitates learning and self-awareness by a review of the behaviour, feelings and interaction of all participants including the worker. He suggests this can lead to 'the most uncomfortable realisation that one's actions are on behalf of one's (harassed) self rather than the client' (p.127).

Personal evaluation Reith (1988) argues that evaluation should be a function of practice. A CCETSW working group (1975, pp.27–32) suggested that evaluating the outcome of intervention was one of seven major functions of social work, and in order to do this the social worker must:

> appreciate the potential value of records and use them for developmental as well as routine (*ad hoc*) purposes
> ... be aware of the need to record the alternatives considered or available as well as the chosen method(s) of intervention
> ... learn to devise and maintain a system of periodic review and reassessment aimed at identifying both the developments taking place and the methods by which objectives appear to have been reached.
> ... must critically evaluate his own interventions and those of others.

However most social workers do not record and analyse their work systematically.

Reith (1988) argues that our failure to evaluate our practice means that we may perpetuate unhelpful interventions without any check and we lose opportunities to improve our practice.

One such evaluation (Lishman, 1978) compared retrospectively my perceptions of my work (as I had recorded them) with clients' views of the services I had offered. This exercise revealed the inadequacy of my records in terms of their vagueness about aims and intervention, the 'clash in perspective' between myself (vague as my recording was) and my clients, and my failure to check whether we actually shared a purpose.

The existence of written records made some evaluation possible but threw into question the value of unsystematised recording which was not shared with or checked out against a client's view.

It is our responsibility to be systematic in what we record and to evaluate how far our aims are achieved. We can also use such records to press for increased resources for clients. However, recording is highly subjective unless checked out with and substantiated by clients.

Worker support   Records can enable the worker to do a better job. Nicolson and Bayne (1984) argue that writing a record after an interview 'helps clarify thinking'. They suggest a structure for recording which includes the following :

- a list of problems;
- the interviewer's thoughts, hypotheses, new perspectives, possible ways of resolving them;
- a note of agreed action.

Coulshed (1988) suggests records can be an '*aide-mémoire*' for the individual worker, particularly as a means of clarifying and recording the worker's thoughts and hypotheses.

However, there are problems inherent in such use of recording. Such 'personal' (to the worker) records have to be distinguished from formal agency records. To whom do they belong? What status do the opinions, perceptions, observations and judgements contained in them have?

While a hypothesis may be helpful in clarifying the worker's thoughts, when put in writing it may lose its tentative, hypothetical quality and stand as a recorded judgement of a client's personality and behaviour. Can such a record be subpoenaed?

Similar concerns may apply to recording in group-care settings. Here recordings, logs or day notes are intended to share information or feedback on key incidents between staff particularly on different shifts. Again, however, comments which may be selective and subjective, when written down achieve unwarranted objectivity and power. For example, a written observation about a resident swearing, may reflect a worker's values about swearing but be taken to imply the resident is behaving aggressively. This selective focus on particular behaviour may begin or reinforce labelling by other staff of the resident as difficult.

There is a problem of confidentiality: who has access to such a day book? What access do residents have to what is recorded by staff about them? What opportunity do they have to challenge staff perceptions and judgements? Similarly where a personal record is kept for each resident, as in fieldwork, what access does the resident/client have to such records? What ethical base is there for a 'personal record' to which the client/resident, whose record it is, has no access?

Payne (1978) raises further reservation about worker records. He points out that marshalling and structuring information does not necessarily lead to improved planning, care, intervention or effectiveness. Planning in records may mean that thinking and planning are not done with the client. Records may serve to disempower clients where information is held and judgements and decisions made without direct access and without dialogue between worker and client.

Gurney (1990) criticises social workers' apparent belief in the crucial importance of gathering (and recording) information about clients and users. He suggests:

> Most social workers seem to operate on the basis that the more they know the more likely they are to be good social workers, to know what they are doing and to retain some control and power over what they do and who they do it to. [He warns] if knowledge is power the more information they have about a user the more likely they are to be in control of their work and the greater becomes the power gap between 'us' and 'them' (p.18).

Gurney argues that such information-gathering is at the expense of assessment and analysis. He argues we should ask 'Is this information relevant to my work? Does it help to progress the task?' If not, he suggests we ignore it.

I have argued that recording (and information collection) has several purposes and that these may conflict. It is important for us to consider always the following questions about recording:

- Who is this record for?
- Who has access to do?
- What purpose does it serve?
- Is the information contained relevant to the purpose?

- Is the information fact, opinion or speculation?

Gurney argues that open access will discipline our use of recording. 'It is a lot harder to collect extensive and useless information in a case file if that file is regularly being read by the user' (p.19).

The following section explores the implications of clients' open access to their files where the purpose of recording is not primarily for the agency or worker.

Client records   The Data Protection Act, 1984, gave people statutory right of access to files held on them on computer. This right of access was extended by the Access to Personal Files Act, 1987, to records held manually in housing and social service departments. Since April 1989 people have the right to see their manual records.

Anyone wanting to see their files has to give notice and authorities have up to forty days to respond. Information about third parties (except professionals) cannot be divulged without their consent (Neville and Beak, 1990).

The legislation reflects public concern about computerisation of records, access to personal files and accuracy and quality of personal records. What values in social work might open access reflect? It implies an open, shared approach with clients where as little as possible is hidden from them. It promotes clients' rights. It involves shared assessment and checked and agreed actions, decisions and records. It was suggested earlier that agency and worker records where information is not shared with clients reflect a position of power and control by the worker and agency over the client. Open access, with its implications of shared planning and decision-making, enhances client empowerment.

Clearly client right of access to records is obligatory. What difficulties can we envisage for social workers in such a policy?

Anxiety that client access may increase staff workloads has been raised. However, Doel and Lawson (1986) found that once workers had developed 'an interactive recording style, using interview time to record the work, the quantity of written material was reduced because it become more focussed'(p.423). A further concern was that clients would not be interested in access. Again Doel and Lawson found 'the support for open access policies was considerable' and they suggested client interest would be greater if workers were more active in sharing records with them.

A major anxiety has been whether social workers' judgements at times need protection and confidentiality. Doel and Lawson (1986) usefully distinguish different kinds of judgements we have to make. 'The first concerns the decision about whether to begin to accumulate information in an investigative manner in order to make a case for legal action' (p.425). Suspicion of abuse would fall into this category and the worker's need to record in terms of accountability and legal evidence has already been discussed. Doel and Lawson accept this limitation to access.

A second kind of judgement is about eligibility for a service or resource, and a third about tentative 'diagnostic' judgements about individual or family functioning. Here Doel and Lawson challenge any need for secrecy or restricted access. 'If you can't confront the client with what you think about then you certainly shouldn't be hiding it away on a record' (p.425).

In Doel and Lawson's study clients were understanding about a worker's need to record, e.g. as an *aide-mémoire*. 'I agree with clients being able to see their files but I also think the worker should have his own personal file, that only he can see, like a top secret file, in effect, that only he sees, no other worker, no other body.' Another client, while accepting the worker's need to record, said: 'I don't mind if other people's views or facts be put in as long as I've got the right to see them and the right to have my views expressed as well, or have it altered' (p.425).

This client's comments again symbolise the issue of power. As Neville and Beak (1990) warn 'the instinctive approach of "doing to" rather than "doing with" clients, which has for so long underpinned workers' attitudes, will be a tough mould to break' (p.17).

In summary, open access means records have to be clear, not jargonistic, well-evidenced, and open to discussion with clients. Social workers have to distinguished evidence from speculation. Records should be used to negotiate a shared purpose with clients. Workers should see recording as a means of communication and intervention and not as residual to their work. Recording should promote partnership between worker and client and promote the empowerment of clients.

These recommendations, although difficult to achieve, are hardly controversial. Difficulties may occur in judging when limited access is required because of the need to accumulate legal evidence, or because some confidentiality between different family members is required.

Agencies and workers need to identify purposes of recording in order to be aware of the times when they are incompatible. They then need fully to understand and adopt a policy of open access, using this as an enhancement of good practice and being aware of when its implementation has to be restricted.

Written communication has been considered in this chapter in only a limited sense. Written communication as a means of direct work is considered in subsequent chapters, particularly in relation to making contracts and engaging in intervention.

4

Building and Maintaining Client–Worker Relationships

The previous chapter examined different kinds of communication. In this chapter we begin to explore the communication skills required for different purposes in social work. While an emphasis on the worker–client relationship has been challenged, because of its inherent lack of purpose, and excessive preoccupation with the process of helping, at the expense of the evaluation of outcome, there is evidence from counselling and psychotherapy, as well as from social work clients, of the importance of the relationship as a means of engaging in collaborative problem solving. It is in this sense, as a necessary base for carrying out social work tasks, that this chapter explores communication skills involved in building and maintaining helping relationships.

The skills examined are those involved in conveying:

- genuineness;
- warmth;
- acceptance;
- encouragement and approval;
- empathy;
- responsiveness and sensitivity.

Genuineness

Genuineness is one of the three core conditions or characteristics found to be necessary (although not sufficient) for a counsellor or therapist to help clients effectively (Truax and Carkhuff, 1957). It is difficult to describe adequately, but essentially it means being oneself. Rogers and Truax (1967) define it as involving the worker in 'direct personal encounter with the client, meeting him on a person-to-person basis'.

Although an essential element of skilled communication in the helping professions, genuineness is not simply a skill to be learned and practised, since it involves our whole self, awareness of self, and ease with self. It is particularly important in showing respect to a client, and as such it crosses barriers of class, gender, race and age. What does it involve?

First, it involves being oneself, without relying on one's role or hiding behind it, expressed by one client (Sainsbury, 1975) as 'I thought they'd be uppity – they were right friendly, as though it were your relation instead of a social worker' (p.86). It involves being open and spontaneous, although as Rogers points out (1980), that does not mean saying everything we feel.

Behaviourally, genuineness involves consistency between verbal and non-verbal messages. Showing verbal interest while tapping my foot suggests my interest is not genuine. In a conflict between verbal and non-verbal messages it is the non-verbal which is usually authentic. It also involves consistency over time, and willingness to recognise one's own inconsistency, e.g. I had to acknowledge to a client whose self-esteem had been low and who had problems in asserting herself:'We've been working on your being more assertive, and now you've just challenged me I've put you down.' Better that I hadn't in the first place, but given that I had, genuineness involves willingness to acknowledge a mistake or inconsistency!

Genuine responses require confidence in the worker's ability to be in touch both with one's own feelings and with those of others, and to feel comfortable with them. If I am embarrassed by tears, for example, my responses will be stilted, and I will give a message to my client that I cannot handle his distress. If I have enough confidence to say 'I feel very sad with you', I convey a message that it is appropriate to have these feelings, and that I can cope with them. One client spoke about how much she appreciated a worker who cried with her when her son was dying. The worker was not out of control, but confident enought to respond genuinely to her client's grief.

Genuine responses require confidence to say 'I don't know' to a client, and then say 'I'll find out' and do so! If I find a client difficult to understand, I need to be able to say so. 'I feel quite confused' is a genuine response to a client's confusion. It may also clarify that the situation is confusing, thus beginning the possibility of trying to disentangle it.

Genuine responses are not defensive. If a client is critical of me or angry with me, I need to feel secure enough not to counter-attack or retreat into self-justification or my professional role. Instead I need to be able to listen, and, if necessary, acknowledge my responsibility. For example, if a client was angry because I had misunderstood him, not responded to something important, or appeared critical, I would need to listen, to acknowledge his anger, and if it was valid to say ' I can see that was not very helpful on my part.'

Genuineness is an essential component of all helping relationships, but it is particularly important with children and adolescents, who, as in 'The Emperor's New Clothes', see only too clearly our inauthentic behaviours – 'She's just putting it on.' 'She's just a fake.'

In residential work, too, genuine responses are essential: as Clough (1982) points out, residential work embraces many of the complexities of family living. Because it is concerned with the whole of an individual's life, it will encompass all the emotions which are part of living – joy, sorrow, fulfillment and despair. It constantly tests the worker's capacity for genuine responses, which may include exasperation, irritation and despondency. Again, genuineness does not involve showing all our natural responses: for example, Clough argues (1982) 'residential workers are not entitled to show all their feelings of disgust and excitement'. However, while it is possible to hide behind roles or tasks (and may be necessary sometimes for self-preservation) the strain of maintaining a false self would be untenable, clearly perceived by the residents, and render the worker impotent to engage in purposeful work.

Genuineness is clearly linked with self-disclosure. Traditionally, social workers were trained to reveal little or nothing of themselves. To clients this lack of response must frequently have felt defensive. We need, however, to think about the purpose of self-disclosure. It should be used when it seems likely to help our client, and not to meet our own needs. 'I am a bit lost – can you go over that again' is self-disclosure which can help the client clarify his or her situation or feelings. Sharing other current feelings, sadness or anger, may also help a client clarify or make sense of his or her own emotions.

Sharing details of personal life can be more difficult. 'How many children have you?' can be a straightforward request to get to know me as a person, it can be a challenge (what experience have you had of child-rearing?), it can be an avoidance (changing from a difficult topic) and sometimes it can feel like an intrusion into my privacy. My responses therefore will vary according to my assessment of the underlying meaning.

Genuineness is difficult to describe and difficult to learn, or, at least, if it is too obviously learned it is not genuine. For me it involves self-awareness and self-monitoring, reasonable self-acceptance, self-confidence, and a willingness to risk trying out authentic responses.

Warmth

Non-possessive warmth, also called unconditional positive regard, is another attribute found by Rogers and his client-centred school (1957) to be a core condition for helping.

Warmth is linked with acceptance, and, like genuineness, conveys respect. It involves the worker accepting the client's experience as part of that person without imposing conditions, and can be thought of as a physical way of showing caring and understanding. It is mainly expressed non-verbally, and for that reason is difficult to define in writing. I know when I experience warmth from someone, but have difficulty putting that into words.

Reece and Whitman (1967) found warmth to be conveyed by frequent smiling, eye contact, leaning forward and absence of finger-tapping. Mehrabian (1972) uses the term immediacy to describe a group of non-verbal behaviours conveying warmth, affiliation and liking. They include physical proximity, leaning towards and turning towards the client, sitting in a relaxed position (although not so relaxed as to appear asleep), maintaining eye contact and smiling.

Immediacy involves physical proximity, but as was discussed in Chapter 3, we vary in how close we like to be to each other and how comfortable closeness feels. We need to be sensitive to the meaning of closeness for our clients. If I stand too close to someone I may seem pushy and intrusive and he will back off. If I stand or sit too far away he may see me as cold and unfriendly. Leaning slightly towards your client conveys immediacy: it indicates attentiveness, and lets the client know you are with him or her. Sitting in a relaxed open position conveys immediacy, but being too relaxed, laid back or slouched may convey disinterest, boredom or lack of respect.

Eye contact is a component of immediacy or warmth, although, as was discussed in Chapter 3, it is also part of regulating interaction and conversation.

Low eye contact can indicate lack of warmth, embarrassment, shyness or fear, and is often interpreted as shiftiness or failure to engage. Looking away in the sense of out of the window or at the clock conveys inattention or boredom. Clients notice it and dislike it. Eye contact, like proximity and position, is subtle, involving a balance between conveying interest, concern and warmth but not becoming intrusive and uncomfortable.

Smiling is an important means of conveying warmth or immediacy. As Sutton (1979) suggests, it 'conveys a positive and friendly feeling, and in biological terms, conveys a non-threatening and benign attitude towards someone who might feel the other person was menacing their territory, their food, their mate or perhaps their self-concept' (p.99). Smiling is also a social reinforcer, conveying acceptance or approval of what it follows. So when we smile to convey warmth and a desire to relate to a client, we also have to be aware that we are rewarding and approving our client's actions and words.

Touch is a means of conveying warmth, and of course, empathy. It means being comfortable oneself with physical closeness, and then being aware of what that means to the client. So, again, using touch is complex. For a sexually or physically abused child touch may be dangerous and intrusive, at least without prior discussion about the child's ability to control the interaction and what happens to his body.

For a bereaved person physical contact and holding is often comforting. I find that in working with bereaved clients some physical touch, shoulder or hand, seems important in beginning and getting 'in touch', although I am not sure why. It may be that it makes contact when the person feels isolated, conveys a physical warmth when the person is chill.

For children in residential care touch, hugs and holding are part of 'normal' parental care which has been lost. We need to be available for a child to snuggle close to when watching television, give and get a bear hug, have a goodnight kiss and cuddle.

For children and adults with severe learning difficulties touch and physical proximity may be essential means of communication, where verbal communication skills and understanding are limited. Touch expresses warmth, affection, reassurance and containment.

The use of touch involves questions of boundaries, appropriateness and sexuality. Touching a client of the same age and opposite sex may be construed as having sexual connotations, as may touch between a young female worker and an adolescent boy. However, to avoid physical contact, or to have fixed and defined rules about it, while helping the worker to feel safer, is at the expense of normal human communication.

A student in a residential unit for disturbed adolescents became uncomfortable with the attempts of one boy to make physical contact with her. She felt there was a sexual component in his touch, and she withdrew from him. She was also aware that he was a child who had been constantly rejected, and that she was repeating this pattern.

She used this awareness to feed back to him her discomfort at the way he touched her. She requested that he stop and respect her boundaries, but at the same time said that she did not want to reject him. After this discussion she and the boy had a closer relationship in which she did not feel uncomfortable and so did not reject him, and in which he was increasingly able to trust her but keep to the boundaries she had set.

Smiling, eye contact, proximity and touch are all essential in conveying warmth, as is spontaneity. However the worker has to be aware of the complex interpretation of these non-verbal behaviours, differing according to culture, gender and individual, and to be sensitive to the meaning of her behaviour for each individual client.

Acceptance

'He was nice – never indicated disapproval or disgust.'

'She didn't sit in judgement.'

'She was never critical, she had a way of putting things which took the guilt away from you, although you knew you were responsible' (Lishman, 1985)

All these clients valued the acceptance and non-judgemental approach the worker showed them, and the last struggled to verbalise how he felt that acceptance by the social worker had helped him to come to terms with his own part in the break-up of his marriage, and, in doing so, to become less depressed.

Acceptance is a rather bland concept, difficult to define except negatively. It is about not 'sitting in judgement' on our clients, and not criticising, praising, disapproving, blaming or condoning. Acceptance does not mean I accept uncritically everything my client does. I do not accept him abusing his child. I hold him responsible for what he has done, and will take action to prevent it. However if I begin by criticising and condemning his child care it is unlikely that we can work together to improve it.

It is in this sense that I see acceptance, a preparedness to try to understand a client's subjective world, without conveying rejection or disapproval.

Encouragement and approval

'I think it sounds as if you've done very well.'

'You know I think all of us can find bits we feel badly about and lose sight of the good bits. Clearly there are lots of good bits in your family' (Lishman, 1985)

Both these statements from social worker to a client convey a clear and explicit positive message of approval or encouragement. Surprisingly in a study of social-worker/client interaction(1985) I found social workers made little use of explicit verbal statements conveying support, encouragement or approval. Mullen (1968) and Reid (1967) in their American studies of worker/client communications found similarly low use of reassuring verbal comments, and they suggested that this was because it was conveyed non-verbally. However it may not be conveyed enough.

There seems general hesitancy or ambivalence in social work about the value of explicitly conveying approval or positive encouragement. This may reflect in part a cultural bias against giving or accepting positive feedback, an anxiety that giving approval can be patronising. It may also reflect underlying values and prejudices in social work.

In social learning theory terms, conveying approval is giving positive reinforcement, defined by Sutton (1979) as encouraging the repetition of good behaviour. Positive reinforcements include tangible rewards, such as money or sweets, or social rewards, such as thanks, praise or appreciation.

As Sheldon (1988) has argued critically, many social workers and educators have in the past resisted using behavioural or social learning approaches. The reasons for such resistance are not entirely clear, but behavioural methods have been criticised for focusing on external symptoms without understanding their meaning for the client, for treating the client as an object and not a whole person, as manipulative, and for giving power to the worker and disempowering the client.

Consciously and explicitly using positive reinforcement may therefore be tinged with anxieties about control and manipulation associated with behaviour modification.

At the same time traditional social worker values of acceptance and non-judgemental attitudes (Biestek, 1965) have been interpreted to mean not only that workers should refrain from conveying their disapproval to clients, but also their approval, since to approve is also to judge.

In reality, in subtle ways, we do manipulate and modify our clients' behaviour, and we need to be aware of the reinforcers we use. Smiling, nodding one's head and leaning forward have been found to act as reinforcers in verbal conditioning experiments, increasing, for example, the amount of speech or the amount of speech on selected topics (Greenspoon, 1955). Brief verbal recognitions (e.g. Hm, hm,) with smiles and positive head nods have also been found to act as reinforcers.

In general clients come to social workers because of problems, and as Nicholson and Bayne (1984) point out, there is a tendency for workers to focus on these. A danger is that we may be selectively responding to problem behaviour and negative circumstances, thus reinforcing their importance in our clients' lives.

Similarly our clients often have low self-esteem and poor self-image, worn down by poverty, ill-health and poor housing; but often attributing the responsibility to personal failure and inadequacy. If we focus predominantly on problem areas we further reinforce their low self-esteem, pessimism and sense of powerlessness.

In contrast the conscious use of encouragement and approval can reinforce positive action and behaviour. In common with showing respect, unconditional regard and empathy for a client, it challenges the client's negative or poor self-concept by giving him/her information (the worker's belief) which is discrepant with his/her own beliefs about him or herself. This kind of 'attribution method' (Miller *et al.*, 1975) has been found to be a more effective way of promoting change than simple reinforcement. The argument is that the worker's belief in the client is discrepant with the client's view of him or herself, and one way of dealing with the discrepancy is to change one's self-image.

If a client with difficulties with her toddler manages on one occasion not to slap and shake her but stays relatively calm, and brings this to the worker, why not praise, approve and say 'That's great. Well done', and acknowledge that achievement. We need to be constantly aware of positive behaviours and change on the part of our clients and give verbal feedback and recognition of them. Keeping an appointment, losing two pounds in weight, paying an instalment on the electricity bill, getting to mother-and-toddler groups can be major achievements for a woman contending with poverty, poor housing, motherhood and depression. Managing not to self-mutilate when his arm splints are removed is a similar achievement for a mentally handicapped adolescent adjusting to community care from large scale hospital or institutional care.

Empathy

'She had the gift of putting things into words. I came feeling mixed. I came out feeling eased and understood' (Lishman, 1985)

This client experienced the value of empathy, the worker's sensitivity to a client's feelings and her verbal ability to communicate this back. Empathy is the third core condition or characteristic found to be necessary (but not sufficient) for a counsellor or therapist to help his/her clients effectively (Truax and Carkhuff, 1957).

In order to be empathic, the worker has to be able to enter his/her client's subjective world, to feel what it might be like for the client, to understand what s/he might be thinking, and to convey this understanding back to the client. The worker has to be able to do this without taking on the client's internal world as his own. That is, I have to be able to understand my client's confusion without becoming confused myself.

Why should empathy be such an important part of a helping relationship? Frequently our clients experience powerful and overwhelming feelings, of chaos and muddle, of anxiety, of anger and rage, of grief and loss. These feelings seem overwhelming not just to the client , but to his /her family and friends, who may then react by avoidance, rejection or criticism. If the worker can convey that s/he understands the power of such feelings, but s/he is not overwhelmed by them, then the client can be reassured that they can be managed and contained.

A woman whose husband died suddenly in an industrial accident was so overwhelmed with feelings of worthlessness, pointlessness and despair that she frequently felt suicidal. For her family this was terrifying, and they could not bear to listen to her distress, instead reassuring her of her importance to them.

My task, as an empathic worker, was to convey to her that I understood that it felt, at this time, as if there were no meaning or purpose for her, that her pain felt unbearable, and that therefore the possibility of suicide offered relief from suffering. However, empathy did not mean that I took on her inner world as my own. While I was in touch with her despair, I did not confirm her perception of suicide as the only solution, but held onto my inner reality of the possibility of change for her. This client stressed the value of a place where she could safely bring any emotion, without fear that it would be avoided or rejected; my acceptance and understanding of the depth of her feelings, without being overwhelmed by them, was part of a process whereby she chose to continue living.

Empathic responses can help a client to make sense of what may feel a jumble of thoughts and feelings. The client may be reassured that there is some meaning in what has felt incoherent, irrational or even crazy. Egan (1986) suggests that to respond empathically we need to ask 'What is the core message this client is expressing?'

Often our clients approach us with anxiety and even suspicion, unsure what to expect, sometimes feeling shame at needing help. By conveying some understanding of how they may feel, we may help them to begin to develop some trust and free them to work on the problems they have brought.

Where a client feels shame or stigma at asking for help, e.g. that s/he should be able to cope with caring for a dementing spouse, conveying understanding of how difficult it is to ask for help and how important it is to be able to cope, may enable the client to think more constructively or appropriately of what s/he can or cannot offer and therefore what services s/he requires.

A client whose son had been stealing and soiling told me much later how terrified she had been that I would simply remove him. For her, most of our early contact was taken up with that preoccupying anxiety. Had I been sensitive and empathic enough to acknowledge that anxiety and her feelings of responsibility and blame, our early contact might have been more effective.

Many families faced with a report for a Children's Hearing or Juvenile Court will have similar anxieties. Even where these are realistic, conveying understanding of how the family might feel at this point may

enable them to share more freely the necessary and relevant information, and possibly, even, become more involved and accepting of the
decision-making.

In working with children, accurate empathy may be an essential tool;
a child or adolescent entering residential care may be overwhelmed by
the size, noise and the group of adolescents. For the keyworker to
acknowledge these feelings, the strangeness and loneliness and the loss
of familiar home and family, will not change these feelings but may
make the transition more bearable.

I am not suggesting that empathy will create open trusting relationships with all clients, but for shared work and problem-solving, a client
has to develop some trust in the worker, and some part of that will come
from a sense of being understood. How many clients fail to return
because they do not experience a worker as understanding their predicament? How many clients in residential care feel isolated, and withdraw
because they do not experience an empathic response from their carers?

Responsiveness and sensitivity

'She listened; she checked out and was fair, so we felt her judgements
were sound.'

'Very perceptive. He gave evidence of how much he had taken in and
how open he is to correction about his mistakes' (Lishman, 1985)

These social workers engaged in checking out their perceptions with
their clients, and were open to the possibility of getting things wrong.
They were not arrogant or blindly insensitive in their interactions, but
showed an ability to be sensitive and responsive to their clients.

Responsiveness can be conveyed non-verbally and verbally. Mehrabian
(1973) found that it was communicated non-verbally by activity:

- by movement: head nods, gesticulation, leg and foot movements;
- by facial expression: pleasantness and changes in expression.

In a study of social work/client interaction (Lishman, 1985) I found
that social workers engaged in surprisingly high levels of non-verbal
movement, in particular of hands and feet, fiddling and rubbing themselves. In general this behaviour did not appear distracting or inattent-

ive, but rather seemed to convey alertness and responsiveness. The social worker who used few non-verbal movements appeared rather wooden, rigid and unresponsive.

Facial expressions conveys mood, e.g. licking or biting one's lips conveys anxiety. Small facial movements have a big impact on the onlooker – e.g. drooping eyelids convey weariness. Facial movement conveys alertness and responsiveness, so that I respond visually to what my client tells me – e.g. smiling at his achievements, looking grave at his problems. Again, in my study of social worker/client interaction, the workers with very few changes of facial expression looked rather like wax models, immobile and unresponsive to their clients.

What is involved in verbal responsiveness and sensitivity? Clearly they are linked to empathy and understanding, but also involve openness, checking out and an ability to seek and receive feedback. There is a world of difference between:

> 'I wondered if you felt a bit that he was taking you for a ride.'

> 'I thought you were saying you were tired of him?'

> 'Have I got that right?'

and:

> 'Obviously you felt he was taking you for a ride and you are tired of him.'

The first, more tentative statements give the client the opportunity to rephrase or correct a faulty impression, and actively checks out the worker's perceptions. The last assumes the worker's view is right.

A social worker has to be aware of the power difference between self and client. How can a client challenge a worker's perception if the worker is arrogant and shows neither respect for nor sensitivity to the clients views? How can a client engage with and trust a worker who appears blind to his or her perspective, who makes untested assumptions about it or who appears unwilling to explore it and negotiate some kind of shared perception?

I work with clients who are male, clients from ethnic groups different from my own, clients of different class and culture, clients of different ages and stages from my own, and with different life experience. I cannot assume my perspective – female, middle-class, middle-aged and Eurocentric – is shared by my clients, but must constantly check, question and negotiate.

If I fail to do this I will be arrogant and insensitive. Further, I will be ineffective. Lack of sensitivity and responsiveness affects agreement between client and worker about the nature of the problem and the purpose of contact. As Chapter 7 discusses, failure to achieve agreement about the purpose of social work contact is linked to poor outcome.

Clearly this discussion of sensitivity and responsiveness is linked with earlier discussion in this chapter, particularly of empathy, and with subsequent chapters on listening skills, purpose of contact and reflection. Being responsive helps to build and maintain a relationship, is a core skill in listening and questioning and is involved in techniques of change, as a component of persuasiveness or social influence.

5

Attending and Listening

In order to understand our clients and their problems we must be able to attend and listen to them. This chapter examines how we may most effectively listen to our clients in the active way which client studies have shown they appreciate.

Preparing for attending

'She was friendly but I got the impression sometimes she was trying to think what was on a notepad in her head, an imaginary one, like to bring out from last week, and not fully listening to us' (Lishman, 1985)

Clients stress the importance of the worker being attentive to them as individuals and they are sensitive to inattention and critical of behaviours which convey it. Attending and listening carefully are important ways in which we convey respect and concern for our clients. How can we convey that we are actively paying attention?

First, ideally we need to prepare to attend to each client, but clearly the context in which we work influences the amount and type of preparation which we have the opportunity to make. In a residential or group-care setting a client or resident may begin to share important facts or feelings and require active attention without warning, e.g. in the middle of household tasks, while watching the television or while going to bed.

A care worker in a residential home for elderly people, was saying goodnight to a resident who,while reading her bible, said 'There have been a lot of deaths recently.' This was the opening for the client to share feelings of loss at the death of fellow-residents and anxiety at the prospect of her own death. For the worker, this remark came out of the blue, and required him to attend immediately to the core message. However, responding to this client required him to delay attending to others. Decisions to attend to one individual in group care have to be taken in the context of the impact on other group members.

In fieldwork settings preparation includes place and purpose. Where is the interview to be carried out: the worker's office, the client's home or some neutral territory? For some clients a visit at home is necessary – for example, a mother with pre-school children or an elderly person with difficulties in mobility may find getting to a city centre office impossible. If we are concerned about child care or a child's development, observation of the child within the home is essential.

However, a home visit is not always appropriate. Violence to social workers is increasing and, if we have any indication that a client is potentially violent, making a home visit alone may be dangerous.

For some clients, an office interview with its anonymity, may be preferred as being less intrusive than a home visit. For some clients, seen on a voluntary basis, attendance for office appointments acts as a gauge of their commitment to contact. For others, seen on a statutory basis, attendance at an office interview is a condition of probation.

If an office interview is chosen, preparation means securing a room and then arranging it, taking into consideration proximity and orientation, discussed earlier in Chapter 3. Putting chairs too close can be oppressive and overwhelming to a client; too great a distance conveys just that. Remaining behind a desk is distancing and conveys a power differential, not conducive to the enabling and empowering elements of social work, inherent even where the authority of the role predominates. Preparation means ensuring privacy and minimal interruptions, even by phone.

We need to consider general areas to explore and be aware of sensitive areas which may be difficult to discuss, e.g. our concern about whether child care is adequate is likely to be met with defensiveness if not anger and hostility. We need always to be aware of the possibility of feelings and issues arising which we did not predict and while we may try tentatively to plan an interview we have to be sufficiently flexible to discard our agenda if necessary and respond to our client's pressing concerns.

We need to be clear about the purpose of contact, e.g. to prepare an initial inquiry report or to assess an old person for residential care. We have to be prepared for other agendas: a family's wish for an old person to go into residential care may not be shared by the old person or even have been discussed with them. We need to be prepared about the kind of information we are likely to need, 'a checklist of areas and topics' (Nicolson and Bayne, 1984), but this should not too obviously dominate the interview as the initial quotation indicates.

We also need to be prepared in ourselves. Nelson-Jones (1983) and O'Hagan (1991) stress the need for self-awareness, in particular, awareness of which situations and topics generate most personal anxiety for the worker, since intense anxiety is likely to lead to inattention, poor listening and inappropriate responses and action. Such anxiety may be realistic, e.g. when a client is drunk and aggressive, but may also be influenced by the worker's own history or experience with previous clients. A student was working with a client with problems with alcohol and was aware of feeling intense anxiety and a wish to get out of the situation which was not appropriate to the particular client or problem. Later in supervision she realised that the anxiety belonged to a previous, but similar contact, where the client had committed suicide. The student had 'forgotten' this very distressing experience until it was reawakened by a client, with almost identical problems.

Our own family histories will affect our responses to current families and situations we work with. For example, experience in childhood of violence by parents may generate intense anxiety and feelings of helplessness, as adults and social workers, when confronted with potential violence. Bereavement in childhood, never talked about, may leave us with intense anxieties about dealing directly with loss.

In order to be prepared to attend and to listen we need to be clear about areas we personally find difficult. My experience has been that by acknowledging and understanding the personal origins of my difficulty, I have been able to attend to and work with clients with similar problems. Awareness of difficulty, however, can also mean realistic recognition of problems one is ill-equipped to work with. For example, if I have recently lost a child by a cot death, illness or an accident, the loss may be too immediate for me to work with others in that situation. In future, however, it may enable me to be more attentive, sensitive and empathic to clients facing such a loss. It is my responsibility to be aware of how functional or dysfunctional I am likely to be.

Attending

Being punctual is an indication to our clients of attentiveness: if we are late it is important to apologise. Lack of punctuality can denote lack of concern.

Once engaged in an interview with the client how do we convey attentiveness?

Egan (1986) stresses the importance of our values and attitudes in attending to the particular client, for example:

'What are my attitudes to this particular client?'

'How are my values and attitudes being expressed in my non-verbal and verbal behaviour?'

Such self-monitoring is an essential component of our ability to attend fully and openly to our clients.

Egan (1986) uses an acronym for the non-verbal behaviour necessary to convey attention, SOLER:

- **S**traight position facing the interviewee.
- **O**pen position.
- **L**eaning towards the interviewee.
- **E**ye contact.
- **R**elaxed position.

These components of attending behaviour are now examined in more detail.

First we need to think about our position. The worker should face the client, as Egan (1986) says 'Squarely': turning towards the client or facing him or her conveys that we are ready or prepared to be involved. We should lean towards our clients at times, again, to convey interest and involvement. Leaning back tends to convey boredom or disinterest although leaning too far forward may be intrusive or intimidating. We need to adopt an open and alert posture. Crossed arms and legs can be perceived as closed or defensive; not open to or attentive to the other's communication.

Being too 'laid back' can appear disinterested and not involved. However we also need to appear relatively relaxed. This means neither fidgeting too much nor being so stiff and controlled that we appear as totally unresponsive. Excessive fidgeting or restlessness can convey nervousness or boredom.

However, too little bodily movement can convey rigidity and lack of responsiveness. Some movement, e.g. occasional shifting of position or leaning towards a client, conveys attentiveness and alertness. Similarly our facial expression can convey responsiveness or disinterest. We need to consider what our normal facial expression conveys, friendliness, anxiety, tension, fear aloofness or disapproval and how much it changes in response to our clients. Complete immobility of body or face is likely to be interpreted as disinterest or even rejection. One client said angrily 'I was pouring out my heart: he never moved and his face never flickered.'

We need to smile: as Priestley and McGuire (1983) suggest 'Not all the time, like a Cheshire cat and not so rarely as a sunny day in November but enough to show that you are awake and listening and also what an essentially nice person you are'(p.36).

Eye contact or looking at the client is important. It conveys that we are attending to the other: it is a way of saying 'I am interested in what you say and feel'. Clearly we do look away at times, for example, when we start a long utterance or sometimes if the material is intensely personal. However, repeatedly looking away can indicate a general difficulty in getting involved or a specific reluctance to getting involved with this person. Either of these responses needs to be explored. Why, if we are in social work, is it difficult to get involved with others? If this is not a general problem, why am I having difficulty in engaging in eye contact with the person? The difficulty may reflect anxieties on our own part, e.g. about abuse or loss or problems on the client's part about sharing, disclosure or intimacy.

Attentiveness is also conveyed by nodding our heads. Again Priestley and McGuire (1983) put it succinctly and humorously, 'No need to outdo Noddy, but gentle, affirmative movements of the head will show that you are following the train of an argument and will encourage further speech'(p.36).

Manner can also convey attentiveness or distance and boredom. It is important, as Sutton (1979) suggests to consider how 'confident, over-confident, tentative, condescending, cold, aggressive, distant or anxious' we appear. Feedback, if we are open to it, comes from clients, colleagues, videos and simulation. Feedback from video indicates that I look anxious whether I am role-playing worker or client. I have had to use this feedback to practise appearing more relaxed than I feel: breathing deeply, relaxing my facial muscles, and consciously adopting a more relaxed posture, including not tensing my hands and fingers.

Listening

Non-verbal attending behaviour is an essential ingredient of listening. Semi-verbal 'following' behaviour is another important component.

Priestley and McGuire (1983) suggest we need to 'grunt'. Like smiling, nodding one's head and leaning forward, brief 'semi-verbal recognitions' like 'a ha', 'mm mm' and 'uh uh' have been found to act as reinforcers in experiments on verbal conditioning (Greenspoon, 1955).

We have, of course, to be aware of the reinforcing element of such 'grunts' and not reinforce behaviour which is destructive to the client or others. Here our own values are important. I am not advocating that we take a narrow, judgemental, moralistic position or that we simply reflect the prevalent social morality and values. Nevertheless I do not think it is helpful to a client to reinforce racist, sexist or other discriminatory views or behaviour or violence and aggression and we need to be aware of when our non-verbal or semi-verbal behaviour is in danger of doing so.

Attending behaviour and semi-verbal prompts are necessary compoments of listening but they are not enough. We also have to follow and understand the client and convey that we are doing so. Active listening in this way is complex and demanding: we have to observe and interpret our client's non-verbal behaviour.

Like the worker, the client conveys attitudes and feelings non-verbally. As we saw in Chapter 3, where there is a conflict between verbal and non-verbal messages (Mehrabian, 1972) the non-verbal messages are generally more important. Again, in Chapter 3, we discussed the difficulties of interpreting non-verbal behaviour. In particular, we need to be aware of non-verbal behaviour 'leaking' otherwise forbidden communication e.g. anxiety, anger or hostility. Egan (1986) usefully summarises the following functions of clients' non-verbal behaviour:

Confirming or repeating: non-verbal behaviour can confirm what a client says.

Denying or confusing: in contrast non-verbal behaviour may be in contrast to verbal utterances, for example, a client may deny anger while his face flushes and his body assumes a tense, hostile posture.

Strengthening or emphasising: non-verbal behaviour can emphasise as well as confirm what is being said. For example, if a client says that she finds a worker's questioning critical and intrusive, and then remains frowning and silent, her non-verbal behaviour adds intensity to the verbal message.

Controlling or regulating: Non-verbal behaviour can be used to control interaction, e.g. if a client becomes distressed whenever a worker begins to challenge her, the worker needs to be aware of this pattern of behaviour.

There are no simple rules for interpreting individual non-verbal signals. It is unhelpful to focus on one single behaviour, at the expense of listening to and understanding the whole person. Non-verbal signals have to be understood within the context of the client's normal non-verbal behaviour.

As well as attending and listening to non-verbal behaviour we have to listen to and understand verbal communication. We can broadly distinguish communication of factual information, and communication of feelings (which may be non-verbal as well as verbal). If we are writing a social enquiry report, a report for the Children's Hearing, an assessment for residential or day care, we have to absorb a considerable amount of factual information. Absorbing such information can be very difficult: to absorb large amounts we need to condense it and organise it into key components. We may need to note down in writing certain factual information but will need to rely on our capacity to absorb and memorise information in order to fill out such notes.

Even where predominantly factual information is being given – e.g. about income and resources – if a client is asking for Welfare Rights advice, feelings emerge – e.g. depression or anger at poverty and lack of help. The expression of feeling demands more of the listener than just an ability to absorb, memorise and feedback what is said. It involves an ability by the listener to get in touch with the client's world at a feeling level and then respond on that basis, i.e. empathically.

Perhaps more useful than a distinction between facts and feelings is Egan's (1986) distinction between verbal communication of experiences, behaviours and affect or feelings.

Clients often describe their *experiences* to us:

'She got mad at me.'
'He's staying out too late for a boy of his age.'

Egan argues that attentive listening to clients' experience is critical for further work: these experiences help us to understand where the client is starting from, his or her frame of reference. While we may wish to challenge this later we have to start there.

We need also to listen to clients' accounts of their *behaviour*. Egan (1986) suggests that describing our behaviour is more difficult than our experience because we are aware of more responsibility for it. Behaviour can be overt or covert. Overt behaviour is that which can be seen by others:

'When he is late I shout at him.'

'When she has a temper I slap her.'

Covert behaviour is about thoughts, attitudes, decisions, memories over which people feel they have some control e.g. planning to stop smoking, deciding to change jobs.

Listening attentively to clients' accounts of their behaviour is again critical: such behaviour may have patterns or triggers of which the client is unaware, or such behaviour may be the focus of quite specific planned change.

Finally we need to listen to clients' *feelings* or *affect*. Sometimes these will be expressed non-verbally, by a defeated posture, by tears or by angry silence. Sometimes they are expressed verbally: 'I feel so down, what is the point of going on?' 'I felt so angry with him, I wanted to kill him.'

Listening and an empathic response are important components in enabling the client to feel that such emotions can be accepted, expressed and lived with and do not have to be hidden or feared. Such acceptance may be the starting-point for a client to learn to live with and manage previously disabling emotions.

However if our listening is partial or distracted, for example, because the client's feelings trigger off our own (about abuse, loss or victimisation) we may convey to the client that such feeling is unmanageable or has to be avoided or is dangerous and unsafe. Such a message, from our poor listening, can only compound our client's feelings of being over-whelmed by and out of control of their emotions.

We need to learn the microskills involved in attending to and listening to clients' experiences, behaviours and feelings, but we also have to listen in a more holistic way. As Egan (1986) points out 'People are more than the sum of their verbal and non-verbal messages. Listening in its deepest sense means listening to the person of clients as influenced by the contexts in which "they live, move and have their being"' (p.86). Such listening involves empathic understanding (considered in detail in Chapter 4). To be empathic we have to put aside our own prejudices and ways of seeing and interpreting the world in order to enter the client's world, and to see things from the client's perspective.

Such listening also involves listening 'for recurrent dominant themes rather than focusing on detail' (Kadushin, 1990, p. 250). Such an ability involves 'listening with the third ear' or as Freud suggested with 'free floating attention'. I have previously argued that having a purpose in an interview aids preparation and attention. However there is a tension between a clear purpose and 'listening with the third ear' and we need to be aware of it and prepare to relinquish the original purpose. Otherwise we may fail to listen and be like the social worker in the quotation at the beginning of this chapter, with a mental notebook or checklist with which we are preoccupied.

Problems in listening

Problems in listening can arise from the setting, the speaker or the listener. A room which is poorly soundproofed allows for outside noise, which is distracting, but also renders client and worker anxious about the possibility of confidentiality. Interruptions by phone or person distract both speaker and listener. Poor acoustics make the task of listening more difficult.

While it is the worker's responsibility to listen attentively some clients' presentation may make this a more difficult task. Sometimes this is not open to change, e.g. if a client has a speech defect. Clients who speak very softly are potentially more able to change. I worked with a woman who initially spoke almost inaudibly. I strained to listen and even wondered if I was becoming deaf. Eventually I explained to this client my difficulty: she was surprised that I thought she spoke softly but then acknowledged that other people had difficulty in hearing her. In time it emerged that her presentation reflected her low self-esteem and feelings that what she had to say was not worthwhile. In a sense I was challenging this belief and conveying that I did wish to hear what she had to say.

A client may slur speech because of drink or drugs. Here, again, telling the client that I am unable to hear him or her properly also conveys a message that I wish to but drink or drugs are impeding me. It may be appropriate to stop the interview and ask the client to return when not under the influence of drink or drugs.

Some clients are rather monotonous: if I find myself bored by a client I begin to feel alarmed. What does my boredom mean? It may reflect a client's low self-esteem, feelings of not being worthy of attention, or depression. Difficulty in listening attentively or boredom signal to me concern: I then have to examine whether the difficulty belongs with the client (low self-esteem, withdrawal, depression) or with me (distraction or defensiveness).

What problems may a worker bring to listening? We have already identified difficulties in being distracted, preoccupied with a previous encounter, or finding ourselves with a client who triggers a painful or unbearable aspect of our experience.

Egan (1986) examines other problems in listening: inadequate listening, evaluative listening, filtered listening and sympathetic listening.

Inadequate listening

Inadequate listening involves being distracted and we have already examined some factors which may distract us. Egan (1986) lists the following additional possibilities:

Physical condition: if we are ill or over-tired our listening skills will be reduced.

Overeagerness/anxiety about performance: if we are too anxious about responding properly we may concentrate on our responses rather than listening.

Attraction: if we find a client very attractive or unattractive this may distract from our full ability to listen.

Similarity of problems: if a client's problems are very similar to our own we may think about our own situation at the expense of the client.

Differences: if the client's experience is very different from our own this may also be distracting.

Evaluative listening

It is difficult to listen without evaluating what the speaker is saying in terms, for example, of good or bad, right or wrong. Such evaluation makes it difficult to empathise and may distract our listening: we need to be aware therefore of our tendency to evaluate while listening. For example, a student working in group care for adolescents, found their swearing so offensive that it prevented her from listening to their very real pain and anger.

Filtered listening

Filters are ways in which we screen information we receive from the world: what we pay attention to and what we ignore.

Filters can be cultural based on class, gender, race, nationality, religion, politics, sexual orientation or life style. Positively, they enable us to classify, generalise and predict. Negatively, cultural filters are likely to lead to prejudice and bias. For example, my experience as a woman, and thereby, structurally discriminated against and oppressed, can render me less able to listen to and understand a middle-class man, who appears structurally to be powerful and potentially oppressive, although privately feels depressed and inadequate after the break-up of a long-term relationship.

As workers, we need to be aware of our potential prejudices: e.g. a student who had felt quite confident in his lack of racism was confronted by his prejudice, the result of years of socialisation, against 'travelling people'.

Finally psychological and social models can act as dysfunctional filters. If I see problems in living as entirely structurally induced, or entirely resulting from interpersonal problems, such a rigid framework will limit my listening to the range of influences (structural and interpersonal) on a client's life, and artificially imposing my model on his or her world. Psychological and social models can help us to organise the information we receive but we should also be aware that they can distort it.

Sympathetic listening

Sometimes in listening to a client's experience, e.g. of abuse, or bereavement, we can become overwhelmed with sympathy. However, sympathy, like bias, can distort: it can lead us to over-identify with the client's difficulties at the expense of helping a client to examine his or her own responsibility and part in the difficulties – the area that potentially can be changed.

Silence

Silence can be one of the most difficult challenges to a listener. Silence, socially, generates anxiety and even embarrassment. Kadushin (1990) points out that a social worker may feel:

a professional anxiety at the thought that continued silence signals a failing interview. It is no surprise, then, that inexperienced interviewers tend to feel uncomfortable with silences and tend to terminate them prematurely. It takes confidence for the interviewer to let a productive silence continue (p.253).

Silence can have different meanings. The client may:

- have said enough on this particular topic;
- need time to think;
- have remembered something and withdrawn;
- have shared highly emotional material and need time to reflect on and deal with it;
- be feeling angry;
- be engaging in resistance or self-protection;
- not saying something which would be very anxiety-provoking.

So, for example, I have experienced clients who were silent because they were overwhelmed with a sudden realisation of feeling from the past, because they were intensely angry with me, or because they became aware of intense vulnerability and dependency on me.

Silence can also be controlling: 'you do something about my pain/problem'. Used in this way it raises anxiety and can be hurtful or discomforting to the worker.

Faced with a prolonged silence we need to interpret what it might be about: if a client is needing time to reflect premature intervention is unhelpful, so we need to decide whether the client needs the silence to be broken. If we are clear that this is so (and not that we are responding to our own anxieties) we can use the following interventions (Kadushin, 1990; Wolberg, 1954). The responses are intended to be tried in the following order.

- Say 'mm' or 'I see' and then wait a moment.
- Repeat and emphasise the client's last word or few words.
- Repeat and emphasise the client's last sentence, or rephrase it as a question.
- Summarise or rephrase the client's last utterances.
- Say 'and' or 'but' as a question as if expecting something to follow.
- Say 'It's hard to talk' or 'You find it difficult to talk.'
- Say 'Perhaps you're trying to think out what to say.'

- Say 'Perhaps you are afraid to say what is on your mind.'
- Say 'I wonder if you are thinking something about me.'
- Even if none of these responses elicits a reply we should 'respect the client's silence and sit it out with him/her' (Kadushin, 1990).

Attending and active listening are essential for engaging with clients, understanding them (and therefore as a basis for assessment) and getting information from them. The next chapter considers more specific techniques for getting information and for giving information.

6

Sharing Information

Sharing information involves both getting information and giving it. As we have seen clients appreciate both: specifically they appreciate active listening, are critical of intrusive questioning and value advice and information.

Gaining information is an essential task in social work, in order, for example, to make an assessment of need or risk, to write a report, to plan an intervention, or justify obtaining resource. It involves attending, listening, exploration, questioning and probing. Giving information is also a necessary task, e.g. about benefits, resources, or client or user rights: it is difficult to do in such a way that the client can absorb the information. It can be done verbally or in writing and can include giving advice.

Getting information

Attending and listening in the ways discussed in Chapter 5 are necessary for a client to feel properly listened to and understood but do not adequately convey our understanding of more complex material. Here more 'sophisticated' verbal responses such as clarification, paraphrasing, making linking statements, questioning and summarising, are necessary.

Reflection and paraphrasing

Reflection and paraphrasing were described in Chapter 3. Reflection involves selecting or repeating a word or phrase a client has used and thereby implicitly conveying an invitation: 'Tell me more about ...' We need to be careful to select something which the client sees as relevant

71

or important rather than something we ourselves find interesting but which seems irrelevant to the client. We can also reflect back to something a client has said earlier and link it with something they are saying now: 'So you feel ashamed now, and you felt ashamed when ...?'

Paraphrasing similarly involves selecting an important issue from what the client is saying but then rephrasing it in some detail and feeding it back. Paraphrasing is hard work and cannot be feigned. If a client says 'That's what I mean' we really have understood what was said. Parroting does not convey active listening or understanding.

Such techniques convey understanding to a client but also check that we accurately understand what the client is saying. Given the prevalence (discussed in Chapter 2) of 'clashes in perspective' between workers and clients such checking-out is essential.

Reflection and paraphrasing need to be expressed tentatively. Consider the difference between:

'I wondered if you felt a bit angry. Have I got that right?'

and:

'You *obviously* were angry.'

In the first quotation the worker reflects her understanding back to the client in such a way as to leave room for the client to disagree or to rephrase what she has said. In the second quotation the worker does not check that she is accurately understanding and she leaves no room for the client to disagree.

Tentative paraphrasing and reflection is likely to facilitate further communication and exploration. The almost dogmatic quality of the second quotation is more likely to close down communication.

Clarification

Clarification means making things clearer. Like selective reflection and paraphrasing it is a means by which the worker can check out and convey understanding to a client. However it is more than simple restating: if a worker successfully uses clarification the client may see a situation more clearly or in a different light.

Clarification also means helping a client to be more specific. A client says 'I've been feeling rather down recently.' The worker clarifies 'In what ways have you been feeling down?' 'When did you begin to feel like this?'

Clarification can be about making clearer rather vague communication. Interviewer responses which begin with 'It sounds as if ...', 'do you mean that ...?' are intended to reflect back to a client what he or she is saying and in doing so to clarify any vagueness. So, for example, a client talked at length in a rambling and disconnected way about different aspects of her life, conveying a vague sense of dissatisfaction. The worker responded by saying 'It sounds as if nothing in your life is very satisfying at the moment: your children seem thoughtless, your husband preoccupied with his work and your boss critical. Life doesn't sound too good.' Here the worker drew together the apparently vague and disconnected negatives and fed back more clearly the client's current unhappiness and the factors contributing to this. By clarifying the worker checked out whether she was understanding accurately but also helped the client to see more clearly that her current mood was depressed and to begin to examine reasons for this and subsequently areas for potential change.

Thus clarification, like reflection and paraphrasing, can involve the worker checking out the accuracy of her/his understanding. Reflection, paraphrasing and clarification are linked but represent increasingly detailed and complex ways of checking, conveying and increasing the worker's (and client's) understanding. They focus on the client's expressed and conscious perceptions and do not attempt to interpret any underlying meaning. Used appropriately and sensitively they are likely to elicit further information from a client. Probing and questioning, used appropriately and sensitively, are also techniques likely to elicit information.

Questioning and probing

Chapter 3 examined the appropriateness of questioning as a technique and highlighted the danger of the worker becoming drawn into an interrogatory question-and-answer routine. It suggested that other techniques, for example paraphrasing and clarification, are equally useful as means of eliciting information.

However, in terms of gaining information questions can help the respondent to tell his or her story, to elaborate or clarify it, and to explore both facts and feelings. The kinds of questions asked can help the respondent to understand what information is relevant to the interview: for example, questions about feelings convey the message that these are important, not just facts. The interviewer's use of questions may help the client to some clearer understanding of what he or she is describing. Questions can help to structure an interview and to focus attention on particular aspects of the respondent's story. Finally, questions can help the respondent to consider alternatives, in terms of understanding problems, and of responding to them, which may lead into contract-setting and problem-solving, examined in subsequent chapters.

Chapter 3 also examined the appropriateness of using different types of questions, open or closed, direct or indirect. While these distinctions are useful it is important to realise that, rather than a dichotomy, there is a continuum of how open or closed, or how direct or indirect questions are.

What are the advantages and disadvantages of each kind of question? Open questions tend more clearly to invite the respondent to share his or her perceptions, views, opinions or feelings openly. Open questions allow the respondent to choose what response he or she will make, and to focus, therefore, on what he or she considers of greatest concern. Open questions communicate that the interviewee carries responsibility for the conduct and direction of the interview, as well as the worker: they set a model of a mutual approach to problem-solving. Open questions are also more likely to elicit information about the interviewee's feelings and intensity of feelings, and attitudes and behaviour. Open questions tend to help people to feel positive about interviews. Their perceptions have been sought and attended to. We saw in Chapter 2 that clients appreciated an unhurried approach, attentiveness, concern and being listened to. Purposeful open questions are more likely to convey these qualities to a client than a rather rigid checklist of closed questions. Clients who valued such an open-ended approach said:

'There was a need to question ourselves, a reappraisal.'

'You've got to realise your whole life is being laid open and this is correct' (Lishman, 1985)

There may be disadvantages in the use of open-ended questions. They may be puzzling or even threatening to interviewees who have had little experience of interviews or who have rigid expectation of structure and guidance. One client expressed this:

'I didn't know what he was after, he wouldn't say. I didn't want to be analysed' (Lishman, 1985)

If a client is unclear about the focus of their problem an open question, 'Can you tell me what brings you here?' may be too vague and more specific questioning may be necessary to clarify what the problem is. Closed questions can help to structure and focus an interview and to elicit further information about specific areas a client has already raised.

In a sense closed questions are a means whereby the interviewer exercises control of what is discussed. So, for example, open questions may allow a client to avoid problematic areas, e.g. around current offences, or around child care and the worker may need to use direct questions to focus on these problematic areas about which he or she has concerns.

Similar considerations apply to the use of direct and indirect questions. As suggested in Chapter 3, by using an indirect question we leave the client greater choice of focus and response. Total reliance on direct questions may be intrusive and lead to a closing-down of interaction and communication on the client's part. However, direct questions may be necessary to elicit specific information or focus on particular areas. Direct or closed questions may sometimes be useful in opening-up a particularly sensitive area which the client is struggling to raise, for example, a disclosure that she has been previously abused either physically or sexually, or that her partner is violent to her.

Probing, which often involves questioning, but also includes paraphrasing and reflection (see Chapter 3) is used to elicit more specific information when a client has been unclear or ambiguous, or where a client has made a rather general or global statement. So, for, example, if a client has been complaining about her child's 'difficult' behaviour the worker might ask 'Difficult?' (i.e. using an accent to probe). 'In what sort of ways?' and if the client replied 'He's always having temper tantrums' the worker might continue 'How often do these occur? Everyday, more than once a day?' and then 'What started the most recent one?' Here the worker is engaged in gaining much more specific and detailed understanding about the child's behaviour. Such detailed probing is highly relevant to understanding what triggers problem behaviour and necessary before the worker and client can move on to identifying possible means by which such behaviour can be changed. Probes can also help clients to identify what aspects of a situation or what specific feelings they find most difficult and to clarify the extent of a problem. For example, if a woman says 'I get quite depressed' it is not clear what 'quite depressed' means. It could range from 'fed up' to 'suicidal' and the worker needs to probe to understand the nature and depth of such an expressed feeling.

We have discussed how questioning which becomes a question-and-answer routine impedes communication. In what other ways may questioning be unhelpful? Overuse of questions can seem like an interrogation and lead to a client feeling threatened and hostile:

'It was like the hot seat, friendly enough, but questions, questions, questions. I was made to feel it was my fault. Others might not go back' (Lishman, 1985)

Kadushin (1990) identifies the following kinds of questions as unhelpful: leading questions, yes/no questions, 'garbled' questions, double or multiple questions and 'why' questions.

A *leading question* is one which is worded in such a way as to elicit the answer the questioner expects or requires. For example, 'You must feel pretty angry about it, don't you?' implies an affirmative answer, as does 'You are feeling better, aren't you?' The use of leading questions can be particularly damaging where clients are considering alternative possibilities and the worker's question suggests or emphasises one view, e.g. 'Do you *really* think you'll be happy in Oaktree Old People's Home?'

Children may be particularly vulnerable to the use of leading questions. 'Your dad hits you pretty hard, doesn't he?' and 'Your dad really loves you, doesn't he?' may each be inaccurate and equally hard, phrased as they are, for the child to disagree with.

Leading questions are least helpful with clients who are likely to agree with what the worker says either because of their need to please and agree or because it is the line of least resistance. Children who have already been subject to abuse of power may have particular difficulty in challenging leading questions from an adult in authority, a further abuse of power.

Yes/no questions are those where the respondent can only answer yes or no. Closed questions are more likely to be yes/no questions. 'Do you play with your children at all?' or 'Are you employed?' imply a yes or no answer. Sometimes this may be appropriate, for example, to gain specific information, for example, about employment. Often, however, questions beginning with 'What?' or 'How?' will elicit more detailed information and open communication, e.g. 'What kinds of things do you do with your children?'

Garbled questions are unclear. They arise from our having a rather complicated or unfocused set of interlinked questions in our minds and in a sense, blurting out the confusion or complexity, rather than clarifying and focusing a set of simpler questions to present. For example, how can a client respond to the following? The baby had required 'special nursery' care following a difficult birth and the worker asked the mother:

> 'You didn't blame yourself, you said. You thought your husband blamed himself, you know. Did he say that to you? Did you blame him secretly? You might not have said yes, maybe it is?' (from Lishman, 1985)

The worker's utterance is confused, includes several questions and it is not clear what the focus is, for example, the client or her husband, i.e. it is garbled. It also includes a leading question, 'Did you blame him secretly?'

Multiple questions, within one utterance, or 'double questions' as Kadushin calls them mean the client is unsure which question to respond to. For example, the worker and client were discussing a baby coming home from hospital and the way in which the mother included the older daughter to try to prevent jealousy. The worker asked, 'So feeding was something she shared in and your husband was still at home, he hadn't yet actually gone?'

Finally Kadushin (1990) counsels against excessive use of *'why'* *questions.* I was struck when someone pointed out that we only use 'why' questions with children in a negative way 'Why did you do/steal/ lose that?' We do not ask 'Why did you do so well?' 'Why' questions, even to adults, may often carry a sense of accusation or at least apparently require the client to justify his/her actions. 'What' questions may be more useful: they probe and require a client to reflect on and analyse behaviour but are likely to elicit less defensive justification. So, for example, rather than saying 'Why did you get angry with your husband?' we might ask 'What was going on just before you got angry with your husband?'

In summary, questions are an important tool in gaining information and in understanding our clients but they should not be overused.

Overuse can close communication, make clients feel interrogated or make them feel they are not getting anywhere.

When questions are appropriate they need to be put simply and clearly, and we need to consider what kind of a question is appropriate; open, closed, direct or indirect.

However, we may need to be careful that our questions are not perceived as critical. This will depend partly on how much we convey the qualities of empathy, warmth and acceptance discussed earlier, and partly on a sparing use of questions and an ability to make use of the alternative techniques identified in this chapter.

Giving information

Our clients are frequently in need of information: about resources, about benefits, about social networks and about legal rights

Clients appreciate being given accurate information when they need it. In social work and in the social work literature its importance sometimes seems underestimated.

Giving information may be a means of helping people to solve problems. For example, information about normal development and behaviour in childhood may help a parent become less anxious, and reduce over-high expectations. Information about dementia may help carers to see problem behaviour as part of the deterioration of dementia rather than in terms of voluntary wilfulness or difficult behaviour on the part of the elderly person.

Giving information to clients can help them to challenge depressing or self-defeating beliefs, by offering a new perspective or frame of reference. Parents who have suffered a cot death may be freed from some feelings of personal responsibility by understanding the general features of the 'sudden-infant-death syndrome'.

Without information about resources, benefits and rights our clients are relatively powerless. With it and ongoing support they may demand and work for rights, benefits and resources to improve their lives. Giving information, therefore, can be an empowering activity. Withholding it or failing to provide it is frustrating and disempowering. Contrast, for example, the experience of the clients in Chapter 2 where the social worker said she did not know anything about the information they requested (Anon., 1973) with the following client's experience of his social worker:

'He's got a lot of knowledge ready at hand that it would take me ages to find out and he knows right away because he's come up against it before' (Lishman, 1985)

Giving information is an important skill but it needs to be done with care. Ley (1977) found that between 40 and 50 per cent of patients did not understand or remember the information given to them by their doctor. This is unsurprising given the short duration of the encounter (five minutes on average:Byrne and Long, 1976), the anxiety of the patient, and the perceived authority of the doctor.

How can social workers ensure that their information-giving is more effective?

Information is more likely to be retained if it is given in the context of a trustworthy encounter so that the skills of engaging and relationship building (Chapter 4) are highly relevant to effective sharing of information.

We need to be sure that the information we are giving is relevant and that the client either wants it or needs to have it. For example, a client may want information about attendance allowance: he may need (although not want) to know the implication of a diagnosis of a child's learning difficulties.

As social workers, we should not give information simply to make ourselves feel better: we should always question who is the information for? Nor should we use information to fill an uncomfortable silence or to avoid a painful area like death or separation. For example, talking about funeral arrangements may be useful and necessary but it can also be used by a worker to avoid confronting raw feelings of shock, anger and pain. Nor should we use information to impose our own values on clients.

Timing is important: we need to give information at the point the client is most ready to hear it. By using skills explored in Chapter 5, we can explore our clients' preoccupations and expectations and thereby give information more responsively, both at the appropriate time and with relevance to the client's needs.

Information needs to be simple. We need to use short sentences and simple, clear words. We need to be explicit, specific and detailed and to give examples wherever possible. We should present information gradually giving the client time to digest it. We may need to repeat it more than once in order to emphasise and clarify it. It can be helpful to ask a client to paraphrase information just given in order to ensure it is really understood. I also find it helpful to check out frequently with my clients whether what I have said is clear and understandable.

It is important to work out with clients how the information we have given applies to their specific situation and how it may be used to solve their particular problem. For example, if an elderly person is requesting information about residential care it may be useful initially to provide information not just about residential care options but also about day care and services offering support at home. It may then be useful to consider how each of these services would apply to this person and what costs and benefits they would each involve. From such information about a range of choices applied specifically to this person's situation he or she may be better able to choose appropriate care, based on cost, suitability and quality.

Finally we need to think about the way that we present information. Diagrams, flow charts or cartoons can be helpful to clients who find it easier to take in information or concepts visually rather than verbally.

Information about services, resources or benefits is difficult to retain if only given verbally. Such verbal information can usefully be followed by clear, simple written information to which the client can then refer at more leisure. If this is a general leaflet it may be helpful if the worker discusses with the client which specific parts apply to their situation and highlights them so that they can easily be re-found.

We should remember that people differ in what helps them to take in information. I prefer information from the written word: others may find it easier to take in in the course of a verbal discussion. As a worker I need to be aware of such differences, and attempt to check out with my clients the most useful way of presenting information to them. In general, though, presenting information in different ways offers a client the opportunity of taking it in in the best way for them and is likely to reinforce the client's ability to take in and retain the information.

Particular consideration needs to be given if the information is 'bad news'. The importance of a trustworthy relationship as a basis for giving information has already been noted but may be particularly important where the information to be given is unwelcome or hurtful or threatening. Here the 'news' may be so disturbing that the recipient finds it difficult to take in, or explicitly rejects it or is hostile to or blames the information-giver.

In order to give such information effectively we need to understand these potential reactions as normal responses to any loss or change which threatens the current meaning of life for the recipients. Parkes

(1975) identified shock, denial and anger as normal responses to the loss of a loved person: Marris (1974) suggests that responses may apply to loss in a wider sense, when a change imposed represents a loss of the previous meaning of life or existence to the person involved. 'Bad news' can represent just this. For example, if an elderly person is faced with the diagnosis that a recent fall is likely to impair their mobility to such an extent that previous independent living is no longer possible, that information represents the loss of their previous way of coping and living and the need for an enormous change. Small wonder they may not understand or reject that news however clearly, sympathetically and skilfully it is given.

Given the normality of denial, anger or rejection of the news, how may our information-giving best aid people to take in unpleasant information? The skills identified so far – e.g. timing, clarity and application – are important. Understanding resistance to the information is helpful. It prevents us from responding impatiently. We can be prepared to take time over several interviews in order that the information is reasonably understood and accepted. Finally if the information is the diagnosis of an illness (e.g. that the recipient is HIV-positive) written information about the likely implications may also be useful.

Written information

We have already noted the value of written information in reinforcing verbal information. Written information, simply and clearly presented, allows a client, as long as he or she is able to read easily, to take in information at an individual pace. It can be a basis for further interviews where discussion and clarification can take place. A further advantage of written information is that it can be translated into the client's first language, either thereby supplementing an interpreter or clarifying an interview where English was used and not translated but was not the client's first language. Social work departments and voluntary agencies have a duty to provide written information in all the languages used by the community they serve.

The skills involved in providing written information are similar to those involved in clear report writing and recording: written communication should be clear, concise and relevant. We need to read carefully the information leaflets we hand out to our clients. Do they make sense to us? Are they clearly written? Do they rely on jargon? Can we more clearly reword them?

Priestley and McGuire (1983) remind us that there are numerous areas of required information which are not available in leaflet form. What kind of information might usefully be presented to clients in written form to supplement verbal discussion? The following are examples:

- Information about legal rights, processes and procedures (e.g. about a children's hearing or juvenile court), the compilation of a social enquiry report, a magistrate's court or a sheriff court.
- Information about legal rights in relation to care proceedings for children.
- Information about different kinds of residential and day care for older people, people with disability or people with learning difficulties (including prospectuses about the establishments).
- Information about residents' rights while in such care.
- Information about agency procedures, e.g. about intake processes or about videoing or screening procedures used in family psychiatry and some child-care teams.
- Information about appeals procedures.
- Information about rights and resources in community care.

Information-giving: other techniques

Not everybody finds written information easy to digest.

Cassettes can provide information orally, but with the advantage that the client can control the speed of information-giving and replay it.

Video tapes can be used to present information. They can be used to present a range of basic information rather similar to written techniques, e.g. tenants' rights, child-care rights and resources, supplementary benefits, job opportunities. They can also be used to present more complex information about processes, procedures or skills, e.g:

- Introducing clients to procedures involved in tribunals.
- Introducing clients to their rights, e.g. in tribunals or in mental health law.
- Introducing clients to procedures and skills involved in job interviews and selection.

- Introducing clients or tenants to means of empowerment e.g. challenging poor or damp housing or inadequate child-care facilities.

Video recording can be used to give information to clients about how they behave and relate to each other in their family or marriage: such direct feedback is information, although it may also provide a means of change.

Information can also be given via *the media*: the local paper, radio or news. This may be particularly useful for people who would not have access to verbal or written information direct from a Social Work Department, who would be eligible for rights or resources but might not see themselves as clients.

Finally, information can be given through *computer information packages*. In Grampian Region Grampian Caredata is a database of local information about services and resources and is available at advice centres and libraries, and the aim is that this availability should be extended, for example, to health centres. The proposals in the Grampian Community Care Plan (1991) for dissemination of information provide a clear concise conclusion to this section on giving information:

> Information dissemination may be by word of mouth, via leaflets and brochures, directories of services, television and radio, newspapers, computer databases, etc. The format which suits one individual may not be appropriate for another ... Account will be taken of the particular needs of visually impaired and hearing impaired people, people with learning difficulties and those whose first language is not English.

Giving advice

Traditionally, giving advice has not been particularly valued by social workers as an activity. Rees and Wallace (1982) quote a probation officer in a study by Rodgers and Dixon (1960) 'We don't *tell* people to do things like that – we'd arrange things if they asked us but we don't tell them what to do' (p.103).

As we saw in Chapter 2 clients valued activity such as advice-giving on the part of social workers as denoting concern and, indeed, construed lack of advice as social workers 'not bothering'. They may also construe failure to give advice as based on incompetence.

Why should social workers appear to be so wary about doing what clients clearly expect and value? Failure to give advice may sometimes reflect the worker's lack of confidence in giving it. I found it difficult to give advice on getting a toddler to bed when I was a newly qualified worker: with my own experience of being a parent I would now feel more confident about exploring strategies and if necessary offering advice.

A worker may be reluctant to give advice because of uncertainty about whether it will be useful to the client, or acted upon. However as Kadushin (1990) points out, even if advice is not acted upon it can have 'the effect of actively engaging the client in problem-solving if only by giving her something specific to react against'.

Finally giving advice may be seen to conflict with client self-determination (Biestek, 1965) although, in reality, this principle is of limited application in certain social work settings e.g. child care or court settings. Maluccio (1979) found that workers in a casework-oriented agency, working with clients with emotional problems, were unsure of the value of giving advice and found it difficult to reconcile with the counselling aspect of their work whose aim, they saw, was to help clients solve their own problems. From this perspective giving advice might increase dependency on the worker and undermine clients' independence and self-determination. However, we should not overestimate the influence of our advice or underestimate our clients' ability to evaluate it and reject it if it is not perceived as useful. Mayer and Timms (1970) found that advice was appreciated if it was similar to that given by friends, relatives or other professionals, i.e. it was evaluated in a social context.

Rather than rejecting advice-giving out of hand how may we use it appropriately? Some considerations are rather similar to those involved in giving information. We should not use it as a means of imposing our values or morals on our clients: it is unethical to advise a client either to have an abortion or not to have one because of our own beliefs. The basis for giving advice has to be the client's request or requirement for it and not as a response to the worker's needs e.g. to be seen to be 'doing' something or to be seen to be competent or knowledgeable.

Kadushin (1990) has some useful advice about the giving of advice:

- It has to be based on professional knowledge and expertise e.g. if it is advice about child care it needs to be based on knowledge, from research or practice, about techniques of child care which are likely to ameliorate this situation.

- Advice has to be given in relation to the context in which the client lives including the social norms of his/her group and how much the advice would be supported or rejected by significant others in the client's life.
- We should only give advice after the client has explored his/her own suggestions, strategies or solutions and again only if the client indicates advice would be useful.

How may we best give advice? Again there are similarities to giving information. Advice is more likely to be taken if it is given in the context of a good relationship, so it is better given later rather than earlier in an interview or series of interviews. Advice needs to be given clearly and simply and the worker needs to check out that the client has understood it. Finally, Kadushin (1990) suggests it should best be given tentatively so that the client does not feel forced to accept it. Given in this way it can be rejected but it can also be a basis for discussion, clarification and even reformulation: the client is then more likely to take on board the 'advised' action and use it positively as their own.

We have seen from studies of clients how differences in perspective inhibit both clients' satisfaction with social work and the effectiveness of it. When we try to gain information or when we give information or advice it is crucial that we try to explain ourselves and to check that our clients understand the purpose of what we are doing. Otherwise our need for information will be seen as inquisitory and rejected and any information or advice we give is likely to be seen as useless and also rejected. All the skills discussed in this chapter – reflection, paraphrasing, questioning, clarification and giving information and advice – are essential to the process of sharing information but all have to be undertaken in a context where the worker and client are clear and agreed about their purpose if they are to be effective. The next chapter explores how we may better ensure that 'clashes in perspective' are minimised.

7

Making a Contract

As we have seen, differences in perception between social workers and clients about what is happening in their encounter appear to be common. More worryingly, lack of agreement between the worker and the client about the nature of the problem and how it should be tackled is an important factor associated with poor outcome (Maluccio, 1979; Lishman, 1985; Fisher *et al.*, 1986).

Given the apparent pervasiveness and unhelpfulness of such differences between the client's and the worker's perspective this chapter explores how we may improve our communications with our clients, about expectations, purposes, tasks involved and interventions required. This is not to suggest that workers and clients will always agree: rather it should be clearer when they disagree.

Clashes in perspective

What lessons can we learn from the numerous examples of misunderstanding between a worker and a client about the purpose of contact in the client-focused research literature?

Mayer and Timms' (1970) original study still has relevance: they identified two major areas where workers and clients disagreed about the purpose of contact. The first area was where a client required financial or material help and was apparently offered psychological or interpersonal help. 'The clients (rightly or wrongly) got the impression that the workers were unaware of their desperate financial need'(Philipps, 1983, p.12). How did this apparent fundamental lack of awareness come about?. While the clients may not have been clear and specific about their need for financial help because of feelings of humiliation and stigma, it is the worker's responsibility to clarify the nature of the client's problem and the worker involved failed to do this.

What are the lessons from this particular clash? Philipps (1983) summarised some lessons. First, the clients' immediate need for financial relief was given early and sympathetic consideration: second, the client, not the social worker made the next move in bringing up other – usually interpersonal – problems and third, the social worker's response to the problems was meaningful to the client.

The second area of apparent misunderstanding and disagreement about purpose of contact was where clients were dissatisfied with the help they received with interpersonal problems. Here the worker appeared to offer psychological insight with a particular focus on understanding the clients' own part in the problem and how they contributed to it. The clients themselves tended to locate it in another, e.g. partner or child, or to want very specific advice and guidance on what to do about it.

This disagreement about the 'cause' of the problem is relatively widespread where clients are seeking help with interpersonal problems, and the belief that the problem lies with someone else and therefore the intervention should be directed at that someone else is particularly prevalent in child-centred problems (Lishman, 1978; Fisher *et al.*, 1986).

How may we better address this clash in perspective? It is less likely to occur if the social worker:

- has been able to engage with the client;
- has shown understanding and empathy;
- has listened attentively;
- if required, has given advice and guidance;
- has explained clearly the purpose of contact and in such a way that the client accepts it.

This last condition may be problematic. For example a social worker who understands family dynamics in systems terms (Coulshed, 1988) will not accept that a child is solely responsible for problematic behaviour although s/he will understand that the parents may perceive the problems in this way. Nevertheless it is the responsibility of the social worker to 'sell' her or his approach and convince parents of the need for a family approach (Gorell Barnes, 1984; Burnham, 1986). It is also our responsibility to be open in defining our approach; one of the concerns about the social workers in Mayer and Timms' study was the impression of a hidden agenda: that they were focusing on 'hidden' problems but without declaring openly their focus.

In child care a similar discrepancy is likely to occur. As Fisher *et al.* (1986) found, 'social workers took as a fundamental tenet that the genesis of child-care problems lay in family relationships rather than in the intrinsic qualities of individuals and sought solutions in "talking things through"'(p.48). If parents were unwilling to consider relationships, social workers interpreted this as 'defensive refusal' and did not explore alternative interpretations, e.g. that the parents felt out of control, unable to influence their children or the situation, and therefore in need of someone else to do so.

Here an assumption is made about the parents' motivation but there is no communication about it or attempt to test it out. Sadly the focus was often on the discrepancy of perception at the expense of areas where the worker and client agreed.

In child care we again see some ways in which social workers contribute to a clash in perspective and probably thereby to a poorer outcome:

- subscribing to a particular model of understanding or solving the problem which:
    the social worker has not explained to the client;
    the social worker has not discussed with the client;
    the client does not understand;
    the client does not accept;
- making assumptions about the clients' motivation which:
    may be wrong;
    the social worker does not communicate to the client;
    the social worker does not check with the client.

Clearly clashes in perspective arise for a variety of reasons, not all preventable, but the major ones appear to involve social workers:

- initially failing to accept and deal with presenting problems, particularly financial ones;
- making assumptions about hidden problems;
- making assumptions about clients' motivation or behaviour;
- subscribing to a rigid model of understanding or solving a problem;
- failing to communicate about these assumptions and models and check them or test them out with the client.

The use of a contractual approach alone will not solve these problems. What is required involves a change in the social workers' value base with increased emphasis on openness, mutuality, reciprocity and partnership, and an increase in social workers' clarity of communication about expectations and means of achieving them. However a contractual approach may offer a discipline to social workers which runs counter to hidden agendas, unchecked assumptions and unspecific or unclear communication of expectations and procedures.

So far we have concentrated on differing perceptions early on in contact. However Sainsbury *et al.* (1982) in a study of long-term family casework found reasonable initial agreement between workers and clients about the purpose of contact, but, in the longer term, workers had more extensive goals than the clients appreciated, usually in the area of family relationships, and rarely disclosed them to clients (a familiar scenario). Sainsbury *et al.* argue that this failure to disclose in the longer term led to difficulties:

- clients did not understand the style of work or the means of achieving the purposes and complained of not knowing what was going on;
- clients complained that the work seemed aimless and they were not clear why the workers were continuing to see them;
- some clients then experienced a decline in morale and failure to deal satisfactorily with their presenting problems;
- workers also complained of aimlessness but for them this involved the clients' 'lack of cooperation' usually in the undisclosed area of meeting further goals.

Sainsbury *et al.* (1982) suggest that a periodic review of the purpose of continuing contact, undertaken jointly, would have clarified the misconceptions they found had developed, i.e. a contractual approach may be relevant not only to initial short-term goal-setting but to the continuing review necessary in longer-term approaches.

Contracts in social work

Davies (1985) defines the use of contracts in social work as involving 'the idea that worker and client shall make an explicit agreement to work towards clearly defined goals'. According to him a contractual approach has the following advantages: 'it encourages honesty in the working relationship; it encourages the explicit identification of some focus for action; and it encourages an element of reciprocity in the exchanges between worker and client' (p.160). For Davies a contractual approach is likely to avoid clashes in perspective.

Before discussing a critique of the use of contracts or identifying the skills involved, some examples of contracts are described.

A female client had been homeless, following physical abuse from her husband, and psychiatric in-patient treatment. She was offered her own council tenancy but arrived for an interview with the duty social worker in great distress saying that she was going to return to her husband because she had no material or financial resources with which to manage her new accommodation or independent life.

The duty social worker clarified the problems:

- no transport to take her furniture and possessions into her new accommodation;
- no bedding;
- no response about a 'community care' grant which would have provided 'comforts' for her new accommodation to ease the transition to independent living;
- anxiety about independent living.

Verbally the client and worker acknowledged the anxiety inherent in becoming more independent. The worker agreed:

- to find transport to take the client's furniture and possessions to her new accommodation;
- to get the necessary bedding delivered from a voluntary organisation;
- to ring to find out about the community care grant.

He discovered the client had not filled in the form, so:

- the client agreed to go to the appropriate office and fill in the form;
- the worker agreed to support the application as urgent in a telephone call.

The worker and client each successfully completed the tasks and the client took possession of the accommodation.

Egan (1986) describes a different kind of contract. A woman's son had disappeared and she became depressed. 'She shunned both relatives and friends, kept herself at work and even distanced herself emotionally from her other son' (p.273). Following confrontation from a close relative and her counsellor about her preoccupation with her own misery she engaged in a series of contracts to 'recommit herself' to her other son, herself and her life. 'For instance, she contracted to opening her life up to relatives and friends once more, to creating a much more positive atmosphere at home, to encouraging Jimmy to have his friends over and so forth. The counsellor worked with her in making the patterns of behaviour clear, detailed and realistic' (p.274).

The use of contracts: problems and reservations

The previous discussion suggests that contracts provide a relatively straightforward and unproblematic means of discussing and resolving clashes in perspective. Inevitably a more critical examination reveals the complexity of issues involved.

1. Underlying the concept of contracts lie assumptions of freedom, choice and self-determination for the client and the worker. In reality these are limited. For example, the worker's 'agency function in probation, child care or mental health ... requires him to use coercion, persuasion or pressure or to have recourse to legal sanctions' (Davies 1985, p.153). Further, Rojek and Collins (1987, p.205) argue that 'the contract approach operates with a concept of freedom that has little application in wider society'. with its contractual inequalities of class, gender, ethnicity and poverty.

2. Underlying the concept of contracts in social work is an assumption, conveyed in terms such as mutuality and reciprocity, of equality between worker and client. Clearly social workers and clients do not have equal power in their professional contact. As Rojek and Collins (1987) point out 'Social workers have accumulated expertise, knowledge and skill through training and work experience. Most clients have not had equivalent experience and cannot draw upon similar knowledge and skills' (p.202).

Neither of these reservations should be taken as dismissive of a contractual approach: rather they spell out the contextual constraints within which contracts are negotiated.

Corden (1980) raises more specific issues about the use and formulation of contracts based on essential features of contracts identified by Maluccio and Marlow (1974) and including:

- *Mutual agreement:* we have seen that disagreement between worker and client about goals or the means of achieving them is associated with dissatisfaction and a poor outcome. However total agreement may be difficult, if not impossible, to achieve. Corden suggests a more limited but realistic definition of mutual agreement: 'that social worker and client can agree a contract even if they disagree quite markedly about the cause and origin of a person's difficulty' (p.152). Corden also suggests 'they might disagree quite markedly about their ultimate objectives in coming together'. This is more problematic: unless open and acknowledged it is reminiscent of the hidden agendas identified by Sainsbury *et al.* (1982) in longer-term work.
- *Clarification of roles:* Maluccio and Marlow (1974) use the term 'differential participation' to refer to 'the emphasis which a contractual appears to place upon clarifying the obligations of the client' (p.153). Corden (1980) argues that this emphasis should apply equally to the social worker clarifying her or his contribution.
- *Explicitness:* this means 'the quality of being clear, specific and open' (p.33). The value of being explicit lies in the avoidance of confusion or clashes in perspective. Corden (1980) questions whether explicitness is always necessary or desirable. 'Some features of interaction between social workers and clients are capable of being acknowledged, appreciated, and understood without being described in the spoken or written word' (p.155). For example, in working with a couple whose daughter had died I made no formal contract beyond saying 'I have come to see if I can be of any help' and making clear to them that grief work was necessary. I cannot imagine setting 'specific explicit goals' and yet in each session there was a focus we all implicitly agreed on and the work of grieving took place (Lishman, McIntosh and McIntosh, 1990).

Clearly contracts are not a panacea for all problems, of communication, purpose and outcome, which arise between social workers and their clients. However they are a means of clarification of expectations, roles, purposes, and ways of tackling problems which may go some way to lessening the feelings of confusion, dependency and powerlessness frequently experienced by our clients.

What are the skills involved in the making of a contract? Initially the worker and client need to discuss the reasons for their professional contact, e.g. the problems the client is encountering, or the resources he or she requires or the legal requirements for contact. Egan (1986) calls this screening and Marsh (1991) refers to it as 'an initial general scan of all the areas that may need help' (p.159). Discussion of these problems or issues requires the social worker's use of engagement skills (see Chapter 4), listening skills (see Chapter 5) and exploration skills (see Chapter 6).

All these skills are involved in the first part of making a contract, what Egan (1986) calls 'helping clients tell their story'. However, the client-focused research literature has shown that while such ventilation or unburdening may initially provide relief for a client, to be helpful and effective it has to lead to something. Here the concept of problem-identification, used in a task-centred approach (Marsh, 1991) (Payne, 1991) is relevant. The social worker will also need the skills of summarising, focusing and negotiation.

Problem-specification

Clients' unburdening often appears confusing and overwhelming both to themselves and the social workers in terms of the range, multiplicity and apparent hopelessness of the problems involved. Following this examination in breadth we need to explore in more detail in order to establish agreement about the major concerns. Payne (1991) usefully summarises steps in the process of problem-specification which are relevant to the formulation of contracts. These include:

- helping clients to describe difficulties in their own way, and then summarising and checking out the worker's perception of the problems;
- trying to reach a agreement about the client's perception of the main problems;
- raising other potential problems, although accepting the client's definition of priorities;
- getting details of when, where and how the problems arise.

Marsh (1991) usefully argues that there are two major factors in prioritising problems: clients' wishes and statutory requirements e.g. about the care of children.

This reminds us of the context in which contracts in social work are made: they frequently reflect a tension between clients' wishes and statutory or social control.

In order for problem-identification or clarification to occur the worker needs to probe, question, clarify and paraphrase. Written techniques can also be useful in helping clients to identify, clarify and prioritise their problems.

Sentence completion

Priestley *et al.* (1983) suggest that the 'simplest and most effective way' of helping a client to identify and clarify problems is to ask him or her to complete the following sentences:

'My biggest problem is ...'

'I also have problems with ...'

While this can be done verbally, it may usefully be written and provide a baseline on which agreement about assessment and possible action may be made.

Brainstorming

Brainstorming is a technique usually used in groups to generate ideas. Priestley *et al.* (1983) suggest it is particularly useful for 'creating lists of concerns'. All ideas are written down, on a blackboard or sheets of paper and the basic rules are:

- as many ideas as possible;
- any ideas, however crazy, are valuable;
- all judgements to be suspended at this stage;
- everything to be written down.

Ideas thus generated can be discussed, discarded, prioritised and acted on. The absence of judgemental attitudes may free participants to be more creative.

While this is generally used in groups it may be a means for an individual to create a list of concerns, or of solutions to problems, freed from judgemental responses normally accompanying such activity.

Checklists

Here the worker may give the client a checklist of problems, e.g. about family, relationships, health, work, and attempt to identify the frequency with which such problems occur, e.g:

	Often	Sometimes	Never
I worry about being overweight	√		
I criticise my boss			√
I chastise my children		√	
I lose my temper	√		

This provides a more private way than brainstorming for a client to review his/her concerns and again may be a basis for discussion and prioritising with the worker.

Checklists can also be used to identify skills, e.g. for employment or in relationships, e.g:

	Often	Sometimes	Never
I show warmth			
I am friendly			
I am assertive			
I write clearly			

This is a useful starting-point for discussion, for helping a client to identify skills he or she would like to develop or for challenging a client: if a client fails to recognise social skills the worker has observed in her or him the discrepancy can be pointed out.

Ranking, prioritising and goal-setting

Once a list of concerns or problems has been drawn up a client can begin to rank or prioritise them both in order of importance and of amenability to change. Again this can be done on paper: a written record of priorities is clearer and better remembered than ideas floating around in one's head. A written record of concerns and priorities can facilitate goal-setting and making a contract and provides a useful baseline to which the worker and client can return both to evaluate progress and keep them to task (Reith, 1988).

For example, a client listed her concerns as debt, being overweight, irritability with her children and poor care of her house. After discussion she was asked to rank her problems and did so as follows:

- debt;
- irritability with children;
- being overweight;
- poor care of house.

Verbally, the social worker requires further skills in order to identify and prioritise of the client's problems: she or he will need to summarise and to focus in order to draw together the client's concerns and to feed them back in order to test out the worker's understanding.

Summarising

The *Shorter Oxford English Dictionary* defines to summarise as 'to sum up' or 'to state briefly or succinctly'. In summarising we try to 'sum up' what the client has been telling us or feed back 'briefly and succinctly' what we understand to be their concerns. Summarising is rather like paraphrasing on a grander scale. It involves selecting out the most relevant and significant themes and issues and discarding the less important ones. It indicates, if properly done, that we have been listening attentively and understanding. Summarising can focus what has been a rather rambling and scattered range of thoughts, concerns and feelings and in doing so give greater coherence and meaning to them. It acts as an overview. It highlights important issues. It can facilitate the transition from exploration to goal-setting, and it can help a client to shift from exploration and ventilation to clarification and thereby a new perspective.

Because of the selection involved in summarising it is important that the social worker checks out that the summary is accurate from the client's point of view.

Kadushin (1990) suggests that mutual participation in summarising is helpful. The worker can invite the client to modify the summary, or to summarise her or himself. 'What would you say are the main issues we've talked about today?'

Nelson-Jones (1983) distinguishes between two dimensions of summarising: reflection and feedback. Reflection summaries involve summarising entirely from the client's perspective: an empathic responding to the client's thoughts and feelings.

In contrast the feedback element of a summary represents the worker's view. It is never adequate alone: it will always be in addition to reflection, developing the client's view; otherwise we are in danger of a clash in perspective again. Here the worker adds an element of interpretation: 'You've been talking about how your family are not supportive enough: they are too interested in their own lives. Similarly your friends are not enough. Perhaps it goes back to your grief; no one is as good as X was.'

Offering feedback such as this may help a client, as Egan (1986) suggests, to develop a new perspective or frame of reference. It can therefore be a useful part of negotiating a contract which involves the client in moving on from her or his current perception of the problem into alternative ways of approaching and dealing with it.

Egan (1986) suggests that summarising can clarify the wider picture, offering a different perspective, and implicitly asking 'What now?' or 'Where do you/we go from here?' This question is an integral part of contracting: it conveys the requirement to shift from a description of how things are now to a focus on what differences are desirable (goals) and how these changes might be achieved (techniques of intervention).

Focusing

Focusing involves prioritising: clients frequently come with multiple, complex problems and focusing is about finding criteria to decide what should be worked on first.

Egan (1986) describes a focusing technique (Rogers *et al.*, 1977). First he asks the client to use one word only to describe her problems, and then put the word into a simple sentence. In working with children, it is not uncommon to ask, as part of the initial assessment, for them to give three wishes. For adults an equivalent is 'What is the main problem just now?' or alternatively, if we focus on change, 'What aspect of your situation would you most like to change?'

Workers and clients can feel bombarded and overwhelmed with problems. Egan (1986) suggests some useful principles about where to start or what to focus on first:

- If there is a crisis deal with it first: a client in crisis will have no spare capacity to deal with other concerns until the crisis has been resolved. For example, a client on the point of eviction will not appreciate a focus on her previous management of rent payment although in the long term her ability to manage it will be crucial.
- Focus on the issues the client sees as the most important. Consider here, the evidence from the client-based research literature where clients had felt the workers did not understand the severity of their problems, particularly financial and material ones.
- Focus on the issues the client is willing to work on: however important an issue in our view, if the client is unwilling to examine it and work on it, pressure to do so is likely simply to alienate them.
- Begin with the problems that seem to be causing the most distress, since the client's motivation to deal with these is likely to be higher.
- Begin with a manageable sub-problem.
- Begin with a sub-problem which is likely to lead to a successful outcome since success in one area can generate success in other areas.

A manageable sub-problem is more likely to lead to a successful outcome, so the last two items are often interlinked. For example, a client was having problems with her 3-year-old who was not sleeping and had frequent temper tantrums. She also felt her husband was unsupportive and that their relationship was deteriorating. The worker and she agreed to focus on the child's behavioural problems and a behavioural programme was drawn up involving 'time out' when there were temper tantrums, and no reinforcement (in the form of drinks, stories or conversation) for failure to go to sleep. The husband agreed with a focus on managing the child's behaviour and agreed to take part in the behavioural programme. The programme was successful: the child went to bed at an appropriate time and had only occasional temper tantrums.

Both parents felt they had successfully cooperated in managing their child's problems and each felt their relationship had improved.

Focusing helps the client and worker to pinpoint both major problematic areas, and areas most amenable to change. However a worker and client will not always necessarily agree on a focus. Here the skills of negotiating are essential.

Negotiation

The *Shorter Oxford English Dictionary* defines negotiation as 'a course or treaty with another (or others) to bring about some result' or 'the action of getting over or around some obstacle by skilful manoeuvring'.

Too often the obstacle in making a contract may lie in disagreement between worker and client (a clash in perspective) about:

● the target for change
● the goals
● the means of intervention

If we take child care as an example the disagreement may be expressed as in Table 7.1.

Table 7.1

Agenda	Client's view	Worker's view
Target for change	The child	The parent or family
The goals	Improvement in child's behaviour	Improvement in family relationships
The means of intervention	Punishment or increased control of the child, e.g. by removal into care	Family therapy as a means of improving communication

Where the contract is voluntary, negotiation appears appropriate to try to find some common ground out of these disagreements. Where legal requirements constrain choice, e.g. in child abuse, negotiation may be irrelevant.

Given a voluntary context how may such fundamental disagreements be dealt with? How can a contract be negotiated? First, we should remember Egan's principles of focusing: if the focus on which the contract is based does not begin with the issues the client sees as most important, and is most willing to work on, his or her motivation for work is likely to be low.

Second, we have to start with and understand our client's perspective: this does not necessarily mean agreeing with it. Rather we need to explore it, accept it as far as possible, and reciprocate by sharing our own perspective and if necessary our disagreement. A major issue from the client-focused research literature was of hidden agendas: perspectives of client and worker were not openly discussed but operated as hidden assumptions which confused and distorted communication. Obviously timing is important as is the skill with which the worker disagrees. If we immediately 'leap in' and 'shout down the client' he or she will be left feeling resentful and not understand.

Third, we need to hold onto and highlight mutual areas of agreement. As Fisher *et al.* (1983) pointed out, in child-care areas of agreement between parents and social worker are more likely to be about *long*-term goals.

Negotiation involves each side being prepared to give: some kind of compromise is reached which is acceptable to each party but not their ideal starting-point. It does involve clarity about the starting-point, and about what is being compromised: it also involves each party being committed to the compromise without feeling short-changed. So, for example, in child care, the worker might initially hope to work with the whole family to improve communication and relationships: the parents, on the other hand might focus on the need for changes in behaviour of one child. The negotiations involved might be complex: the social worker might accept the desirability of the child's changed behaviour, the child might demand more positive reinforcement and attention from the parents and the parents might have to accept any behavioural change on the part of the child would involve them heavily in administering the programme and giving reinforcement to improved behaviour.

Sometimes negotiation may be unsuccessful and a contract may not be possible. This may be because the worker does not have the resources, e.g. financial or material which the client requires. Here it is important that the worker is honest and does not string the client along. It may also be helpful to acknowledge the validity of the request even though the worker cannot respond.

The discrepancy between the goals of the client and the worker may be too great. If the parents require behavioural change in a child without any willingness to be involved themselves a social worker may feel pressure to collude in a scapegoating process and thereby unable to form a contract. If a family want residential care for an elderly parent but the elderly person does not agree, and is not at risk, a contract may not be possible.

The discrepancy may be about means of intervention: if a group of tenants want to deal with the issue of damp housing by exposure of the landlord and protest demonstrations against him, and the worker would wish to begin by establishing channels of communication (i.e. a conflict model versus a collaborative one) a contract between tenants and workers may not be possible.

Sometimes a worker will be unable to enter a contract because of the agency's reluctance to allow her or him to engage in any activities which might be seen as political or jeopardise sources of funding.

Contracts can be limited or constrained by the legal framework, and mutuality, reciprocity or negotiation then play little part. For example, the social worker's use of legal authority in relation to the protection of the children will predominate

However, even in this setting the expectations of parents can be clearly and explicitly set out, and choice promoted where possible.

Working with resistant or reluctant clients

Not all clients who are involved with social workers have chosen the involvement: as indicated some encounters are constrained by statutory requirements. Does reluctance or resistance to contact render contracting impossible? Rather we should consider how we may attempt to work with such clients.

Egan distinguishes between reluctant clients, people who have been more or less forced to come, e.g. because of a supervision or probation order, or when dragged along by a spouse, and resistant clients who may have referred themselves or overcome initial reluctance but 'balk' at the implications of the work at some point.

Egan (1986) gives examples of reasons why people may be reluctant and/or resistant to help, including the following:

- seeing no reason for going for help in the first place;
- feeling resentful at third party referrals, e.g. in child abuse it is common for the parents to express anger that the referral was mistaken;
- fear of the unfamiliar;
- uncertainty about expectations;
- ambivalence about change;
- seeing no advantage in change;
- once change has started seeing more costs than benefits
- feeling that having to come for help involves weakness, failure or inadequacy, 'losing face'.

In what ways may we most usefully respond?

- it is important to acknowledge the client's feelings of reluctance rather than deny them, and to explore them;
- it is important to discuss what is going to be involved in the contact;
- it is important to be clear about the limits of our responsibility;
- it is important to see that resistance is usual;
- it is important not to view resistance as deliberate ill-will or a personal rejection If we think instead of 'avoidance' we may more productively think of why the client needs to use it and what incentives might help him or her no longer to need it;
- it is important to examine our own resistance: the more we understand our own the more we can understand and help our clients;
- it is important to examine our own behaviour: are we eliciting resistance? Sometimes a hostile client can elicit our defensiveness or get under our skin in such a way that we attack in return;
- it is important not to attack resistance, rather to accept it, respect it and work round it. Egan (1986) says 'befriend the resistance'.

The use of a contractual approach, while realistically not a success with every client, may by its emphasis on openness, shared decisions and participation help resistant clients to feel more engaged and more in control of the process.

Conclusion

The use of a contractual approach can facilitate greater clarity between worker and client about expectations, goals and means of intervention and thereby reduce the risk of a clash in perspective. However it is not a panacea for all problems between workers and clients.

In particular differentials in power between worker and client mean that the relationship is unequal and may reduce the opportunity for mutuality and reciprocity. However contracts are not a unitary phenomenon: the context and purposes of social work vary enormously and influence the potential for contracts.

Some clients are highly motivated to seek help, in some ways know what they require and see that as legitimate, and see themselves as partners in the helping process (Rees and Wallace, 1982). For them contracts may be a natural means of negotiated mutually agreed roles and tasks. Other clients may be more reluctant, or may feel stigmatised and powerless at having to seek help. For them mutuality in contract making may be more difficult but the clarification of expectations, of goals and the ways these might be achieved, via a contract, may be a means of increasing their commitment to the process and increasing their sense of power and choice. Some clients have no choice about their contact with social work: they are legally required to do so. The contract then is not mutual: it defines the expectations of the clients and their failure to comply may result in legal action. The main value here is that it is, at least, clear to the clients specifically what the requirements of them are. As one client said 'This was the first time she'd known what the agency expected her to do before she got her children back' (Salmon, 1977, quoted in Davies, 1985, p. 162).

Contracts are perhaps most clearly seen as useful in crisis, task-centred or behavioural work: here the problems to be addressed are clearly defined, the goals clear and specific, and the tasks discrete, specific and incremental. The task-centred model involves a commitment to partnership in the sense of a respect for the client's view, a great deal of effort being put into good communication, a preference for joint actions on problems, and a recognition of the abilities of the client where appropriate (Marsh, 1991).

However a contractual approach is not limited to these models: it can be appropriate in counselling, and a psychosocial model and in working with families and groups (Coulshed, 1988). Its value lies in the discipline it requires of workers in terms of clear communication, of clarification of expectations, of negotiation of mutually agreed goals and therefore a mutual commitment to the work, and of discussion and negotiation about how the worker and client may best achieve the goals. It carries the implication of time limits but they do not necessarily limit the work to short-term goals and approaches: the use of a contract, short-term work, periodic review and evaluation and a further contract can be useful in longer-term work in reducing client and worker aimlessness. As already suggested, an explicit contractual approach may not be helpful in certain social work contexts, e.g. working with the dying or bereaved or in admission to residential care for an old person. However the principles of a contractual approach can still usefully underly practice, e.g. in clarifying expectations, discussing the purpose of contact, or considering 'where do we go from here?'

A final question is whether contracts should be written or verbal. The value of a written contract is that it is explicit, open equally to worker and client and neither can deny it at a later stage. Writing down the problems renders them concrete and may be the first stage of a client confronting and taking responsibility for them.

Sometimes the problems and issues to be worked on may appropriately be less specific, e.g. ventilation of mixed feelings. Here a written contract may be too concrete and simplistic, running the risk (Corden, 1980) of devaluing the significance of what is being shared. For example, a key worker and a 12-year-old boy in residential care drew up a written contract:

1. defining desirable and unacceptable behaviours;
2. setting out realistic goals for the reduction of unacceptable behaviours;
3. defining the consequences (withdrawal of particular privileges) if the goals in 2) were not achieved;
4. defining rewards for performance of desirable behaviours.

The definitions, goals and consequences were mutually agreed.

Simultaneously the key worker and the boy had an informal, verbal agreement that he had access to the worker whenever she was on duty for half an hour before his bedtime. He regularly availed himself of this time and used it to talk about home: in particular, his distress after his mother's death, and his anger that his father did not seem to care for him. In this second case the contract is implicit but apparently mutually agreed on: a written contract or even a more formal explicit verbal contract seems almost too crude to address the delicacy, depth and sensitivity of this child's agenda.

Contracts can often help to prevent the clashes in perspective outlined at the beginning of this chapter, and, while they are not always relevant to every social work encounter, the awareness and conscious use of a contractual approach is a useful discipline for the worker in ensuring that she or he clarifies, checks out and negotiates with clients about the purpose of contact.

8

Intervention: Non-Verbal and Verbal Techniques for Changing Attitudes and Behaviour

Both client-based research (Maluccio, 1979) and social work theory (Milner, 1982; Sheldon and Baird, 1978; Fischer, 1978) have been critical about undue emphasis in social work on the relationship or process at the expense of effectiveness or outcome.

Writers such as Sheldon (1977) and Fischer (1978) argue that social workers should concern themselves with the evaluation of the effectiveness of their intervention. They stress the importance of:

- thinking about the ends of work, not just means, i.e. goals and outcomes;
- setting specific goals to avoid a double agenda, diffusion of goals, inactivity and lack of change, and failure to offer what the client wanted;
- developing and definiting intervention skills for problem-solving and change.

Such a focus on effectiveness does not deny the importance of relationship building, but the relationship is the means of engaging in collaborative problem-solving, and not an end in itself. Fischer (1978) argued that the worker to be optimally effective must:

- establish trust and a caring relationship;
- employ techniques of change.

We have already seen that social workers in all settings need to build relationships with their clients and to enable them to tell their stories. Sometimes the combination of empathy, active listening, probing and clarification may be enough to help a client to gain a new perspective on his or her problems and to engage, without further intervention, on problem-solving.

More frequently, offering clients a supportive relationship and the opportunity to unburden is not enough (Maluccio, 1979) and intervention skills aimed at problem-solving and changing attitudes and behaviour are essential.

What skills and techniques have been found to be effective in promoting change? In psychotherapy Orlinsky and Howard (1978) found that active and positive participation by the therapist is linked with positive outcome. Leading, rather than reflective behaviour, confrontation, praise and direct approval are all more likely to lead to a good outcome.

In social work the findings are slightly less clear and integrated, but Reid and Hanrahan (1981) found the following factors to lead to greater effectiveness:

- the use of focused intervention methods;
- the adaptation of behavioural approaches;
- contract-based programmes;
- careful matching of client and target problem with a particular style of intervention.

This chapter examines intervention skills which may increase a worker's effectiveness in helping clients to solve problems or make changes in their attitudes or behaviour.

First, however, we must address the question of whether personal change (of attitudes or behaviour) is a realistic and valid goal of social work. Two strands of argument are particularly relevant:

- is change of any kind (personal, social or political) a valid aim of social work?
- is personal change a valid aim given that most clients' problems lie in the structural arenas of poverty and discrimination?

Davies (1985) is critical of the emphasis in social work literature on change, personal or political. He argues that a more realistic goal is maintenance: 'maintaining a stable, though not a static, society, and maintaining the rights of providing opportunities for those who in an unplanned uncontrolled community would go to the wall'.

It is not appropriate here to engage in a critique of Davies's essentially consensus and pluralistic stance: rather we should note and consider his questioning of the validity of aiming for change in social work.

Radical social workers, in contrast, do promote the concept of change in social work but the change involved is of the system and not of the individuals. Radical social work 'challenges social work's preoccupation with individualistic explanations of social problems. Such notions are condemned for pathologising the poor/deviant victim and devaluing the role of collective political action and self-help in the attainment of humane welfare provision' (Langan and Lee, 1989). From such a perspective, attempting to help an individual to change ignores the powerful structural influences defining her or his situation and problems and runs the risk of 'blaming the victim'.

Both the radical social-work perspective and the pluralist maintenance perspective are relevant to the context of any discussion of skills involved in bringing about change for individuals. Many changes which social workers and their clients would wish to bring about are not within their control: for example, relief of poverty, reversal of unemployment, provision of adequate housing and removal of discrimination on the basis of race or gender. It is important to be clear in our assessments what problems are structural in origin and outside our clients' and our own individual abilities to change. It is also important that we make clear to our clients that these problems are outside their personal control and responsibility: being poor is not the fault of the poor person or his or her 'poor' management. It reflects a social and economic structure in which unemployed people or people in low income jobs are completely inadequately resourced to live their lives (Becker and MacPherson, 1988).

To assume that we can help clients to change or solve these problems is unrealistic or even arrogant: the solution is political. However as social workers we cannot ignore the impact of poverty and discrimination on our clients' lives. How may we address it? Langan and Lee (1989) stress that we need to work in a more structural and adversarial way: in particular we need to challenge 'attempts by the authorities to promote the idea that poverty is a problem of personal failure, rather than a social problem'.

We need to acknowledge with our clients the social, political, economic and structural pressures which disadvantage them, and to promote collective action. We need to work in ways which are empowering and do not individualise structural problems.

However, many clients do bring problems to social work which they would like personally to solve or to manage better: the law or social work may face them with problems they need to manage better, for example, child care or offending behaviour. For them, acknowledging their structurally disadvantaged position or promoting collective action to address it may not meet their current individual needs. Negotiation about goals within their personal control may enable them to manage current problems more effectively. Changes in behaviour and attitudes, in this context, are ways of problem-solving within the reality of a disadvantaging and discriminatory social structure.

This chapter and the following one examine non-verbal, verbal and written communication skills and techniques which may be useful in work with clients around change and problem-solving. They are not concerned with models of social work practice (Coulshed, 1988; Payne, 1991): the skills involved are relevant to a range of intervention models.

Underlying this chapter is the assumption that a social worker is a source of influence and persuasion for clients: that where the social work task involves helping clients to change, the process must involve the social worker's use of influence to promote that change.

What is important about influencing is to know when we are doing it. We need to be aware of when we reinforce other people's behaviour, when we slip into giving opinions, when we may be trying to control our clients: if we are aware of how and when we are influencing we can use this more responsibly and more openly to achieve goals agreed with our clients.

Non-verbal influence

Chapter 3 examined non-verbal behaviours and explored the impact of social workers' non-verbal behaviour on clients. It was suggested that non-verbal communication is extremely influential: where there is conflict between verbal and non-verbal messages it is the non-verbal ones which predominate. It was also suggested that there are problems in interpreting or decoding non-verbal behaviour: one behaviour can convey more than one emotion, clusters of behaviour can convey a different meaning from each individual behaviour, and the meaning of non-verbal behaviour may vary according to culture and to context.

Are there non-verbal behaviours which may be influential in terms of the focus of this chapter, changing attitudes and behaviour? Status and power, responsiveness, persuasiveness and reinforcement may all be conveyed non-verbally and are relevant to exercising influence.

In Chapter 3 we saw that people of higher status tended to adopt a more relaxed posture (involving leaning sideways, a reclining position and asymmetrical placement of limbs) and it was suggested that adopting a relaxed posture may convey our assumption of status and power. Sitting behind a desk or in a higher chair also signifies higher status or greater power: sitting in the lower seat can feel quite disempowering and disabling. Finally power or status can be conveyed by an 'expanded' bodily posture with an expanded chest, erect head and body and raised shoulders, and low power by a bowed head, dropping shoulders and a sunken chest.

We need to consider how much power we do wish to convey non-verbally. If we are engaging in a partnership with the client with an emphasis on mutuality and reciprocity, assumption of unequal power will be inappropriate, counterproductive and ineffective and a complementary posture and seating arrangement (similar height chairs arranged at right angles) should be chosen.

Sometimes, however, it may be relevant to convey power non-verbally. It can reinforce the use of firmness and authority of the kind Sainsbury (1975) defined, which included instructions to carry out specific tasks, demanding certain kinds of behaviour from clients and even exercising moral pressure i.e. it can enhance very direct guidance and influence which is sometimes required and appreciated by clients, 'They've got to be strong. They should be able to take control of the situation' (Sainsbury, 1975). When we are giving advice or guidance (see Chapter 6), for example about child management, the assumption of power non-verbally serves to strengthen and emphasise our verbal message thereby increasing its influence.

Responsiveness is an ingredient of the non-verbal behaviours Mehrabian (1972) found to be involved in persuasiveness and influencing people. In Chapter 3 we saw that responsiveness is conveyed by activity involving bodily movement, facial expression and quality of verbalisation, including longer communications, unhalting quality and faster speech rate.

Immediacy is another element of persuasiveness, involving shorter distances between people, more eye contact, moderately relaxed posture, and frequent head-nodding. According to Mehrabian, responsiveness has the most powerful persuasive effects although immediacy has some lesser persuasive effect.

A final non-verbal means of influence is reinforcement. As we saw in Chapter 3 smiling, nodding one's head, leaning forward and brief verbal recognitions (e.g. mm … mmm) act as reinforcers of opinions or attitudes.

According to Argyle (1978) the following kinds of behaviour have been influenced by these reinforcers:

- amount of speech;
- opinions;
- speech on particular topics;
- non-delusional speech;
- favourable self-references;
- leader activity.

Argyle concludes that: 'operant conditioning of verbal behaviour, and probably of other behaviour too, is an important process of influence in dyadic encounters. The effect is rapid and can occur without the awareness of the person influenced. It may also occur without the knowledge of the influencer ' (Argyle 1978, p.179).

It is important that we are aware of when we are using reinforcing non-verbal behaviour and that we do not use it indiscriminately or to reinforce undesirable behaviour. More positively we can consciously use such reinforcers to encourage attitude or behaviour change. In working with a client with very low self-esteem I have been aware of reinforcing non-verbally any statement where she expressed a positive attitude to herself, and of nodding furiously and approvingly when she told of an instance where she had been able to assert herself at work.

Verbal techniques

Some of the techniques discussed in earlier chapters on relationship-building, sharing information and making a contract are also means of intervention to promote change, e.g. empathy, reflection, clarification, questioning and probing, giving advice, summarising and focusing. In this chapter they are re-examined as potential ways of helping clients change and problem solve. We also look at a new technique, challenging, which specifically addresses the task of helping people to change their attitudes or behaviour.

Empathy

Empathy was defined and its use explored in Chapter 4. How can its use help clients to solve problems or make changes?

Empathic responses can help a client who is stuck to move forward. Feeling understood and having problematic feelings and experiences accepted can help one to leave them behind. A frail elderly man had several times begun the process of applying for residential care and then withdrawing. He again approached the social work department. The worker explored his current situation and then commented that it sounded as if he had very mixed feelings about such a move. She was able to convey to him her understanding of his current need to be cared for, but also his apprehension about dependence and his feelings of loss, of his independence, his home and, in a way, his past. Taking time to explore and acknowledge these feelings, and the empathic responses with which they were met enabled him to move on to a positive decision about his need for greater security and care and a decision which he did not subsequently regret.

Empathic responses can help to validate and confirm a client's perceptions which previously have been ignored, disqualified or disconfirmed. While this cannot 'heal' or solve the past hurt it may reduce its power in the present by helping the client to recognise the hurt and live with it, and perhaps 'lay it to rest' and move on.

A young woman had been mutilating herself. Her self-esteem was low and she had had a series of relationships which had always ended in rejection. She talked about her mother whom she had found powerful and controlling but who had also helped her practically and financially. She mentioned that as a child, whenever she had tried to touch or embrace her mother she had been pushed away. The worker said how hurtful and rejecting this must have felt: the woman looked surprised and then relieved and agreed. The worker's empathic confirmation of the rejection she had felt (but which had always been denied by her mother) began a process whereby she acknowledged that her mother had been rejecting but that this was not her fault. The worker's empathy and confirmation of the client's perceptions helped her self-esteem to rise a little and she began to see connections with her current difficulties.

In residential or group care empathic responses can be an important means of intervention. Here workers have to be able to respond to critical incidents or significant statements by residents as they arise, without preparation. If we can convey empathic understanding of what the resident is trying to convey this may be therapeutic whereas simply to respond to the overt behaviour or words may leave the resident feeling that he or she has not been understood and that real communication is not possible.

An elderly resident, in an old people's home, who was seen as bitter and disagreeable, was complaining to a worker about the food and the other residents. The worker neither ignored her nor rebuffed her but acknowledged how difficult she seemed to be finding life in the home. The old lady began to talk about how difficult her life had always been, particularly as a child when she felt her parents had preferred her younger sister. The worker commented on how upset and angry she seemed to be feeling and how hard it must have been as a child to feel less loved. The old lady spoke with great distress about how she had felt that no one understood what she had gone through. Over time she talked more about her life with the worker and while she was still perceived as a rather difficult person some of her bitterness seemed to be alleviated.

Reflection and clarification

Reflection and clarification are not only a means whereby the worker checks out, conveys or increases her or his understanding of the clients' problems. They are also a means of helping clients to develop new perspectives about their situation, an essential component of problem-solving and change.

A client arrived at an intake team in considerable agitation. She poured out an almost incoherent jumble of problems and the social worker felt quite overwhelmed. She reflected this feeling back to the client and wondered if the client felt like this too. She then began a process of trying to clarify the major problems or concerns. Gradually the client began to identify three problems which concerned her most: debt, her husband drinking and her children being out of control. The worker used further clarification to establish concretely and specifically:

- what debts were owed;
- when the husband drank;
- how the children behaved.

What emerged for the client was that the debts were the main problem: whenever a demand for payment or a bill came in the client felt overwhelmed and depressed, the husband went for a drink, and the children's behaviour deteriorated. The client decided that the problem she wished to address with her husband was the debt management; the worker agreed to a limited contact with this focus, to negotiate on the client's behalf manageable repayment schedules, and to explore the possibility of charitable help.

A young probationer left his work because he felt he was being picked on by his foreman. The probation officer clarified exactly what the foreman had done and said, and the probationer began to realise how touchy he was about any feedback even if it was constructive criticism.

Questioning and probing

Like clarification and reflection, questioning and probing may enable a client to gain a new perspective about a problem. Skilful questioning and probing involves the client in examining his or her attitudes, values, perceptions, and assumptions, and, in a sense, defending them or revising them.

An enraged father appeared before the duty social worker asking for his teenage daughter to be taken into care. His only concern was that she was involved in a relationship with a young Chinese boy at the same school. The worker used probing techniques to examine what this concern was about, and the following picture emerged. The father had no worries that a sexual relationship was involved. The boy's family was prosperous and united, integrated within a predominantly white neighbourhood, although prominent members of the Chinese community. As the father responded to the worker's probes, his anger and anxiety appeared increasingly unrealistic and prejudiced and he left, more accepting of his daughter's choice and aware of his own stereotypes, although with continuing anxiety about the development of the relationship.

Probing for what is missing as a client tells a story is important as a means of intervention. A resident in a centre for people with physical disability was describing with amusement being asked to leave a pub. The worker probed about the reasons: the resident had been told that in a wheelchair she was a fire risk. The worker probed further about whether the resident thought that was true or the real reason, and the client identified prejudice and discrimination as the probable reasons for exclusion. The worker probed further: what had the resident felt? The resident said she was used to it, but on further probing said it was hurtful and made her angry. The worker and she then looked at whether she could use these feelings to try to change the situation. They agreed to go back to the pub together and jointly try to educate the publican and challenge his prejudice.

Giving information and advice

Sometimes a client may not be able to deal with a problem because of lack of relevant information or misinformation. New information can lead to a new perspective.

In working with people who have experienced loss or bereavement I have found that giving information about normal reactions, e.g. about anxieties about going mad or 'seeing' the lost person, has helped clients to accept that this is what has to be undergone, and reassured them that they are not crazy: while this does not relieve the pain it frees the bereaved person to tolerate the processes of grief without additional anxieties, and to be more prepared to face the pain rather than try to avoid it.

Where parents are presenting problems in dealing with their children's behaviour, giving them information about normal child development and behaviour at different stages can be helping in providing them with a new perspective. Temper tantrums, bed-wetting or difficulties in getting to sleep are examples of behaviour which parents often see as problematic and deviant and try to punish or eradicate. Information about the normality of such behaviour at certain ages can relieve parental anxiety that the child is disturbed or the parents have gone wrong. They are then more open to considering alternative ways of responding to normal, if irritating, behaviour.

Practical information can help clients to solve problems. Information about the use and availability of a bell and buzzer can help a child and parents to deal constructively and effectively with a bed-wetting problem. Information about respite care and sitter services can help the parents of a child or adult with severe learning difficulties in decisions about care. A parent who feels desperate and overburdened by the demands of basic care may reluctantly contemplate long-term residential care: provision of information about alternatives may lead to more effective decision-making and problem-solving where the parent gets respite from the demands without the necessity of what would have felt like rejection.

Giving advice is an explicit social influence technique and an intervention which can contribute to clients' problem-solving. In Chapter 6 we looked at considerations involved in deciding whether it was appropriate to give advice. In particular we have to be careful that the advice is not simply a reflection of our own need to feel useful or of our values, but does respond to a client's need for some structure and direction.

Giving advice effectively can only be done when we have established an influence base (Strong, 1968) and when clients expect and are receptive to it (Mayer and Timms, 1970; Maluccio, 1979).

As Kadushin (1990) says: 'We are expected to have some knowledge, some expertise, about social problems and the variety of alternatives to their amelioration. We are supposed to have had some repetitive experience with the probable consequences of the various solutions available. All this gives the social worker the legitimate grounds for offering advice' (Kadushin, 1990, p.173). Our advice should come from knowledge, expertise and experience.

There are different degrees of directiveness and explicitness in giving advice. 'I think you should do X' is more directive than 'Have you thought of doing X?' but each can be relevant and useful. If I am working with a client who is depressed and not eating or sleeping I will say, 'I think you should go to your GP' and I will follow that up to try to ensure that the advice is taken. If a client is having problems with benefits I will say, 'I think you should go to the Welfare Rights office' and I would ring to try to arrange an appointment. Explicit, directive advice can be empowering for a client. If a client was being sexually harassed at work I would say that I think she ought to contact her Union and consider formal complaint procedures. I would advise equally directively if the client was suffering racial discrimination.

In other circumstances I would use a more tentative form of advice. For example, if a carer is becoming increasingly worn down by looking after an elderly frail parent, I would say 'Given how frail your mother is, have you thought about a nursing home?' If a parent is complaining about a toddler's temper tantrum I might ask, 'Have you ever thought of ignoring it?' or 'Have you ever thought …?' and describe the use of time out.

Summarising and focusing

Summarising and focusing are intervention skills as well as ingredients of making a contract (see Chapter 7). They also give a client new perspectives on his or her situation and provide 'leverage' on problem identification and solving (Egan, 1986) by helping a client to identify and prioritise major areas for change.

When we summarise effectively we feed back to a client his or her story but in a selective way, highlighting what we see as major issues. This selection is a form of influence.

So, for example, a parent has multiple concerns about her 4-year-old son's behaviour. The worker selects and summarises: 'So you are worried about lots of aspects of Jack's behaviour but it seems to me your main concerns are:

- first, he nips the baby;
- second, he won't go to sleep at night and comes into your bed;
- third, he has temper tantrums when he doesn't get his own way.'

Here the worker selects from an overwhelming catalogue of complaints what she perceives as the major concerns and in doing so renders the problems more discrete, specific, identifiable and thereby manageable. The client begins to sense that the problems are not completely uncontrollable and selects the failure to go to sleep as the most immediate one to address. The change is her feeling that the problems are not insoluble but that she and the worker can jointly begin to identify ways in which she can manage them.

Focusing, similarly, can reframe complex and overwhelming problem situations by identifying and selecting the major concerns. Focusing can also identify themes, e.g. rejection, loss, discrimination or dependency which may underlie a myriad of apparently unconnected presenting problems. For the client to realise that a theme is persistent and recurrent may offer a different perspective on current problems, which begin to make sense in the light of past experience. As importantly, with that understanding, the client may put aside the 'emotional baggage' of the past and be freer to deal more competently with here-and-now problems.

A woman client was extremely self-critical and lacking in trust in herself and others. Over time she brought numerous problem situations where her negativity sabotaged her own actions and abilities and her relationships. The worker focused on the theme of her harsh self-criticism and excessive demands of herself and others. This focus brought home to her the pattern of her behaviour and she began to explore what had led to it. Gradually she became able to stop herself being so self-critical on significant occasions and was more able to live with herself.

Interpretation

Interpretation involves more than reflection or clarification: using these techniques we stay within the client's frame of reference. When we interpret, however, we extend or challenge that by using alternative frames of reference to suggest explanations of behaviour or attitudes.

Kadushin (1990) says: 'A clarification or paraphrase or reflection stays very close to the message as presented. Interpretation takes off from the message and includes a inference derived from it, one added by the interviewer' (p.155).

Interpretations do involve inference: they will vary according to theoretical orientation. A structural orientation would emphasise structural influences, e.g. poverty, gender or ethnicity or behaviour. A psychodynamic orientation would stress the unconscious influence of the past on present attitudes and behaviour. A cognitive orientation would emphasise the influence of faulty cognitive processes on behaviour. These orientations are not incompatible; both outer, structural influences and inner emotional and cognitive influences affect behaviour.

An interpretation from a different perspective can challenge a client's current perspective, attitudes or behaviour. For example, a colleague working in an intake team with clients who predominantly are poor, interprets their current difficulties as structural: this challenges their conviction that poverty is their personal responsibility and due to mismanagement. This structural perspective frees both worker and client to be more realistic about financial management, in particular about prioritising. It does not solve the problem of poverty but it challenges personal responsibility and guilt.

Interpretation involves making connections for clients: between apparently random current behaviours, between thoughts, feelings, attitudes and behaviours which have not previously been seen as connected or between past influences and present attitudes and behaviour.

Interpretations are conjectures or hypotheses but we have to be careful to make them on the basis of sufficient information. Otherwise they are simply random guesses. They have to be made tentatively, since they reflect *our* perception which may not tally with the client's view of what is wrong or needs to be changed. In my own research on social workers' behaviour I found that they varied enormously the way they offered interpretation. Some appeared arrogant: failing to check that they were understanding correctly or putting comments in such a way as to override the client and leave no room for disagreement, e.g.

'You *obviously* felt inadequate in that situation.'

Others checked out that they were understanding or put an interpretation more hesitantly or as a question, e.g.:

'It sounds as if, perhaps, you felt rather inadequate.'

Interpretations which are pure guesses or leave no room for disagreement are likely to lead to clashes in perspective, whereas tentativeness and checking-out reduce the risk.

To be effective in problem-solving an interpretation has to be seen as valid by the client. Kadushin (1990) suggests it has the 'greatest probability of acceptance when it is within the grasp of the interviewee "sensed but not yet clearly understood"'(p.158). It is more likely, therefore, to be effective if it introduces only a slight discrepancy from the client's view of the situation.

Winnicott (1971) conveys clearly the importance of the client's perception of how valid an interpretation is. 'An interpretation that does not work always means that I have made the interpretation at the wrong moment or in the wrong way and I withdraw it unconditionally' (p.9).

Clients can disconfirm workers' interpretations either by disagreeing or more commonly ignoring them. An example of outright disagreement is (Lishman, 1985):

Worker: 'That's a secret you have from your husband.'

Client:'No, I tell him everything.'

More dangerous in that it is more likely to lead to a clash in perspective is when a client ignores an interpretation and the worker assumes it is accepted.

A more successful interpretation occurred when a worker made a verbal link between a mother's current anxieties about her 8-year-old son's behaviour, including soiling and stealing and her residual feelings about her brother who had the same name as her son and had been a bad lot and ended up in prison. The mother began to see that her anxieties about her son did not belong to him and were more about the past. She also saw that she might be engaged in a self-fulfilling prophecy: the more anxious she was about her son's behaviour the more he behaved in ways which justified her anxiety. As she began to see her son more realistically his behaviour improved.

Challenging or confrontation

Challenging and confrontation were defined in Chapter 3 as ways of feeding back to a client discrepancies in his or her behaviour, thinking or feelings.

Reid (1967) defines confrontation in a similar way to interpretation, as explanations or formulations designed to help the client to become aware of the nature or meaning of patterns of response in his or her behaviour, attitudes or feelings in relation to:

- the worker–client interaction;
- the client's functioning in family roles;
- the client's functioning in social roles;
- the client's normal behaviour and attitudes.

In my own analysis of social worker's behaviour (Lishman, 1985) I defined confrontation as 'statements which face the client either with behaviour of which he/she is not aware, or which he/she wishes to avoid looking at, or with some discrepancy in his or her behaviour between words and deeds, attitudes and behaviour'.

For example, a social worker confronted one probationer as follows: 'What if I say to you that behaving as you did almost sounds to me as if you were asking to be taken back inside' (the probationer had been on a stealing 'binge' and then given himself up to the police).

Egan (1986) stresses the importance of challenging in helping clients to change and solve problems. He suggests it can involve the following:

- stimulating awareness of relevant experiences, attitudes or behaviour;
- feeding back clients' incomplete interpretation of experiences, behaviours or attitudes;
- feeding back to clients their lack of understanding of the consequences of their behaviour;
- feeding back discrepancies in clients' lives, e.g. between attitudes and behaviour;
- challenging clients when they hesitate to act on their new understanding.

In these different ways of confronting or challenging we are facing clients with contradictions, distortions, inconsistencies or discrepancies and inviting or stimulating them to reconsider and resolve the contradictions. While such a reconsideration does not in itself change behaviour, the readjustment of interpretations and attitudes involved is likely to lead to behavioural change. The ultimate goal of challenging, however, is action and change.

We now examine some different components of challenging: stimulating awareness, exploring and outlining consequences of behaviour, challenging discrepancies, distortions, self-defeating thoughts and omissions and challenging clients about hesitancy to act.

Stimulating awareness

We are all sometimes unaware of our behaviour and its impact, our thought-processes and our feelings and these blocks may be a major contribution to our problems. If shyness is presented as aloof behaviour it may be difficult to make relationships. If we think (faultily) that whatever we do is doomed to failure we may never start anything. If we feel unlovable or lacking in self-esteem we may withdraw from relationships, or fail to pick up any positive messages from other people. Stimulating awareness may be about behaviour, thoughts or feelings.

- *Behaviour:* if a client trusts the worker and values her or his opinions the worker's feedback about how the client behaves or presents may be a useful challenge. I worked with a young woman who had very low self-esteem and very little trust in other people (for good reason). Over time she began to trust me and gradually I was able to feed back to her how suspicious and hostile she had initially appeared to me. She was able to see that she did behave like this with new people and that it was threatening and offputting to them. This awareness helped her to change her behaviour: quite consciously she practised and began to give more positive verbal and non-verbal messages, even to new acquaintances and she found them reciprocated. Videotapes and audiotapes can also feed back to clients their presentation and behaviour. However, care has to be exercised: to use a video to feed back to a depressed client their negative presentation is likely to further reinforce the depression. In contrast, to show a rather abrasive client the impact of their presentation may help her or him decide to modify it.

- *Thoughts or cognitions:* faulty or irrational beliefs or cognitive states can lead to problems of anxiety, depression, negative self-esteem, and general inability to problem solve. Ellis (1962) suggested that often people have ways of thinking which keep them locked into their problems: we can call these self-limiting or self-defeating thoughts. Dryden and Scott (1991) summarise these self-defeating thoughts as follows:

  - I must do well or very well! I am a BAD OR WORTHLESS PERSON when I act weakly or stupidly
  - I MUST be approved or accepted by people I find important
  - I am a BAD, UNLOVABLE PERSON if I get rejected
  - People must treat me fairly and give me what I NEED
  - People who act immorally are undeserving, ROTTEN PEOPLE
  - People MUST live up to my expectations or it is TERRIBLE
  - My life MUST have few major hassles or troubles
  - I CAN'T STAND really bad things or very difficult people
  - I NEED to be loved by someone who matters to me a lot.

  When we pick up evidence of these ways of thinking we can question them or challenge them by providing an alternative more rational belief.

- *Feelings:* our clients sometimes bring to us horrendous stories of loss, deprivation or abuse. Quite often clients present these appalling histories with little affect. They have learned that certain feelings, e.g. anger or sadness, are unacceptable to parents and must never be expressed, or that they are so vulnerable that expression would have little point. However, hidden or 'repressed' anger at persistent abuse or deprivation is likely to affect current functioning: it may lead to depression, low self-esteem, or inability to sustain relationships and a general unease with the emotional or relationship aspects of life. I have found it useful to feed back an emotional response, 'Listening to your story makes me feel extremely angry' or 'extremely sad' and I always mean it. Often clients look quite shocked, but my response stimulates them to think back to how they might have felt: it gives permission to experience feelings they have repressed. Similarly it can be useful to say, 'Often, in your circumstances, people feel X.' Again this introduces the possibility of hidden or forbidden feelings and the normality of experiencing them.

Finally it can sometimes be useful to say, 'You have told me about your childhood but it is almost as if you have no emotion. If your daughter (aged 8) told you she was being treated in this way what would you feel?' Putting the client into a more distanced position of a child other than themselves may help them to experience feelings on behalf of a vulnerable other which really belong to their own childhood.

- *Missing thoughts or feelings:* here we draw attention to what is important but avoided or left unsaid. Kadushin (1990) gives an example: 'To the client who was referred for counselling because of neglect of her children and who spends the first twenty minutes of the interview consistently talking about the rise in the cost of living, the interviewer might say directly: "I think we both are aware that we are together to discuss your care of the children. We would need to begin to discuss that now"'(p.162).

- *Incomplete perception or interpretation:* here we sense that the client is seeing things in a very limited or incomplete way. For example, an adolescent girl had run away from home and complained of her mother's nagging and very restrictive rules. The social worker examined the mother's expectations in more detail: gradually the girl began to acknowledge that the restrictions arose from the concern about her safety and were not punitive or intent.

Helping clients to explore consequences of behaviour or actions

Here we invite clients to explore, or confront them with, the potential consequences of what they choose to do. Exploring the likely consequences of a range of decisions is a means of making decisions based on predicted outcomes. A client who was pregnant was discussing the options of termination, adoption or keeping the baby. Although she was in a long-term relationship with a partner she made no mention of him. The worker questioned this and invited her to think of the consequences of a decision made without consulting the baby's father, her partner.

Exploring consequences may be very important in work where we carry statutory authority. Probationers who do not turn up for supervision need to be confronted with the consequences of their action: recall, a court hearing and potential imprisonment. Similarly where we have concerns about child care we have to confront parents with any failure to meet conditions of supervision and its consequences. For example, failure to be available weekly for meeting with the social worker, and failure to have the children at nursery on a regular basis will result in an early review children's hearing and the possibility of the children being taken into care.

Challenging discrepancies, distortion, self-defeating beliefs, games and excuses

- *Discrepancies:* discrepancies occur between verbal and non-verbal behaviour, between what we think or say and what we do, between our own views of ourselves and others' views.

    Often we are not aware of discrepancies and here challenges may provide useful feedback and the opportunity of choosing our behaviour.

    The worker may comment on discrepancies between verbal and non-verbal behaviour. A client maintained that he did not see the value or purpose of becoming angry: he always maintained calm. As he spoke he looked and sounded more and more angry and became quite flushed: the worker pointed out the discrepancy between what he said and how he looked. The comment led him to think about why he found it so important not to be angry and the impact on his family (with whom he was having difficulty) of these rather mixed messages.

    We may challenge statements which do not seem consistent with normal behaviour. For example, a woman said consistently that she never felt angry with her children. The worker challenged this by expressing surprise: never to feel angry seemed unusual for parents! Again this led to exploration around anger, and the woman gradually became more able to express anger to her children and set appropriate boundaries: in response their behaviour became more manageable.

    We may challenge a client's perception of self: 'You see yourself as funny: other people have been saying you are sarcastic'. We may challenge when a client says one thing and appears to do very differently: a man protested how much he cared for his wife and children but the worker challenged how little time he seemed to spend with them.

    Finally we may challenge discrepancies in a very positive way. A client may present a catalogue of failures and disasters. In contrast the worker is aware of considerable strength and achievements and feeds these back. 'You say you've achieved nothing. Over the last six weeks you've told me about your bonus at work, your son getting an apprenticeship and you and your wife having a night out for the first time in ten years and enjoying it. Is that nothing?'

- *Distortions:* here the client finds it difficult to see other people in realistic ways. A young man had been brought up by a powerful domineering grandmother. In relationships with women he always experienced them as overpowering and critical. The (female) social worker observed this pattern and fed back to him how he always interpreted her remarks as critical. This made her feel quite helpless and powerless. Her perception was a direct challenge to his distortion of her. He was taken aback and then began to examine when and how he interpreted her comments and distorted them. This began a process whereby he more often perceived women more realistically.

- *Self-defeating beliefs:* we examined these earlier in terms of raising clients' awareness of when they were engaging in self-defeating beliefs.

  It is also important for the worker to challenge a client whenever he or she slips back into self-defeating beliefs, even having become aware of them. For example, a mother felt responsible for everything in her family and that she had to do everything and do it right: not surprisingly she felt exhausted and depressed. She was aware of her self-defeating beliefs but still got caught in them. The worker challenged, 'There you go again, expecting 100 per cent of yourself and punishing yourself when you don't quite make it. What about the 99 per cent done well?'

  The more we pick up on and challenge clients' self-defeating beliefs, the more likely they are to be aware of when they are beginning a self-defeating sequence and to challenge themselves out of it. Clients can use thought-stopping (simply refusing to think about the particular negative set of thoughts) or self-talk (talking oneself out of them) as a means of self-challenge. In working with a client with a very self-destructive history I always picked up statements about his badness, worthlessness and unloveableness, fed them back to him and challenged their accuracy in the light of his current behaviour and performance. Gradually he took this on board for himself: when he started to think such self-defeating thoughts he would question or challenge them or practise thought-stopping until his current pessimistic mood had passed.

- *Games:* Berne (1964) identified 'games people play' in relationships and interactions: the games have a manipulative element and the danger is of getting hooked into the game, and thus being restricted in one's ability to help. One game is the 'Yes, but' game where a client presents as helpless and desperately needing the workers' help, advice and guidance, but then deskills the worker by conveying that whatever she or he offers is ineffective: there is always a 'but'!

  Initially we have to set up a climate which discourages clients from playing games. For example, in the 'Yes, but' game we are more vulnerable if we present as the expert, whose wisdom is then never quite right. In contrast if we are clear that responsibility for the problems and their solutions lies with the client the 'Yes, but' game is less effective.

  Sometimes however a client will persist in attempting games even if the atmosphere is not encouraging and we have to challenge the games playing. A very passive young man would present his difficulties and problems to me, look helplessly at me and then sit and wait. If there was a silence he would look helpless and wait for me to fill it which initially I did. I began to feel I was doing all the work and I challenged him the game I felt he was attempting to hook me into of 'Rescue me'. I saw this as a game he played in other aspects of life, taking little responsibility but then feeling resentful at other people taking over. Within sessions I refused to 'rescue': we sat out some long silences and he began to be more active in considering his difficulties and potential ways of managing them.

- *Excuses:* we all make excuses for ourselves at times, but excuse-making can be problematic if it leads to avoidance of problems or disowning responsibility. Excuses leading to avoidance include complacency, 'It won't happen to me', and procrastination,'It doesn't need to be dealt with now' (Egan, 1986). Both need to be challenged as ways of avoiding problems or problem-solving. They are no basis for work or changing attitudes or behaviour or problem-solving.

  Disowning responsibility is expressed by 'I'm not the one who needs to act' (Egan, 1986). This is often expressed when there are problems in relationships, e.g. between parents and children or in marriages, and has to be challenged, if there is to be work to improve the relationships. One colleague, when faced with a parent or spouse, who said 'It's not me … it's her/him' would say 'It takes two to tango' and then go on to set out the way he worked: that a breakdown in a relationship was the responsibility of each person involved. The task now was to work on ways where each person could contribute to improving it.

Challenging can be an effective way of helping clients to reconsider attitudes and behaviours and to change them. However it always needs to be done with care.

Challenging can only take place on the basis of a good relationship. The client has to trust the worker and to feel properly understood otherwise a challenge may be heard as a criticism. Challenges are better delivered tentatively like interpretations: they are then more likely to be seen as a basis for discussion rather than a criticism. We must combine challenges with understanding and empathy. The client needs to feel that the worker is 'with' him or her and the challenge is based on positive regard and a realistic appreciation of the client's difficulties and potential for change.

Challenging strengths rather than weaknesses is more effective (Berenson and Mitchell, 1974). This means challenging clients with their assets or resources, which they may not recognise.

Challenging or confrontation is not criticism, putting clients down or making them face things: these are unethical and will arouse anxiety, hostility and defensiveness.

Good challenging or confrontation arises out of our concern and respect for a client, our understanding of their predicament, and our desire to help them to deal more effectively with their problems. Kadushin says 'The best confrontation mirrors the Bible's admonition to "speak the truth in love"'(p.166).

9

Intervention: Written Techniques for Changing Attitudes and Behaviours

Intervention techniques

How can we use written techniques in helping clients to solve problems or change attitudes or behaviour? As we discussed previously, putting things in writing makes them concrete. Words spoken can disappear: we forget or lose what seemed important in a previous interview. Writing things down can be a way of holding onto difficult or complex attitudes or feelings while they are being worked on and can make it difficult to avoid them. If we write down promised actions, the paper represents a commitment (although we can, of course, tear it up!). It also is a means of review. If we write down strong or forbidden feelings we are more likely to acknowledge them and face them: in talking they can drift away. Sometimes a client may write a letter to a worker in order to share difficult feelings or experiences e.g. about abuse or sexuality which he or she would find too threatening to begin to explore face to face.

Written techniques can help in the following areas: decision-taking, changing attitudes, monitoring and changing behaviours and dealing more effectively with feelings, or with the past.

Decision-taking

Clients can be encouraged to use brainstorming (see Chapter 7) to generate ideas about action to bring about change or solve problems. Brainstorming is a creative activity where all ideas, however crazy, are written down and judgement is suspended. It helps to free client and worker from the tramlines of conventional thinking which clearly have been limited so far in solving the problems that the client is bringing. It can generate a feeling of enthusiasm or hope. A woman was moving out of psychiatric care into an unfurnished flat. She had very few possessions and very little money. She brainstormed possible ways of getting furnishings and appliances: her list included the following:

- take out a loan;
- rob a bank;
- ask friends for the contents of their attics;
- apply to social services;
- go to the minister;
- ask her sister to lend her some money.

While we do not judge ideas when they are being brainstormed because this inhibits creativity, once the written list is complete the client can begin to evaluate the ideas. Some will be discarded as wild or impractical but from the reduced list the client can begin to weigh up pros and cons of each action in order to decide the most feasible and potentially effective. Here the client is evaluating the potential actions in terms of his or her priorities and goals, and if a decision is reached it will be owned by the client and not imposed.

A useful way of evaluating potential actions is to draw up a list of costs and benefits for each. A client was offered a job several hundred miles away and was confused and ambivalent about whether to take it or stay where he was. The worker encouraged him to draw up a list of costs and benefits for each alternative action: his list is presented Table 9.1 overleaf.

How we weigh such a list of costs and benefits will depend partly on temperament and personality. If we value change and excitement they are likely to outweigh a number of costs: similarly the importance of security outweighs other costs.

Finally, in deciding on actions it can be useful to write down a time-scale for doing this: this has to be realistic but writing down *when* we will do things acts as a pressure to do them. 'I will go to the Job Centre on Tuesday' holds more commitment than 'I will go to the Job Centre.'

Table 9.1

Option	Costs	Benefits
Moving to take the job	Distance from family Homelessness ? Housing Unsure whether I can do it	More money Challenge Opportunity to make friends
Staying in current job	Boring Lower pay Loneliness	Security Near family Know what I'm doing

Changing attitudes

In the previous chapter we discussed self-defeating beliefs. Writing is a very useful way of challenging them. For example, I often ask such clients to write down a list of the good things about themselves. Sometimes I give this as homework and ask them to bring it back to the next session. Sometimes I ask them to do it with me in the interview. Frequently clients will say how much easier it is to write down the negatives and even ask if they can do this. Sometimes they have to do so before they can start on the positives and the written list of negatives can be used to examine the client's perception in more detail and challenge them. Some clients really struggle to find positive things about themselves or if they do disqualify them:

'Well, I work hard but it makes me irritable.'

'I am a good housekeeper but I shout too much at the children.'

It is important to acknowledge how difficult this task is but also to suggest it may represent some of the problem and to hold the client to it. I would question and prompt in order to remind the client of what I perceived as his or her strengths. Sometimes when clients have completed this as homework they have come back with a sense of achievement:

that somehow forcing themselves to think of their positives had helped them to own them and believe them.

Monitoring and changing behaviour

In order to apply a behavioural approach the worker together with the client has to identify which behaviours are most problematic and distressing, but also which are most amenable to change. They also need a baseline as to when and how often undesirable behaviours occur. Recording such a baseline may be by using a graph or, as Sheldon (1988) suggests, by diaries, kept by clients in which they can record 'both occurrences and reflections'. Sometimes the act of recording baselines can in itself be helpful. To discover that a problematic behaviour, e.g. an adolescent shouting at a parent (which has come to assume major proportions for the parent), in reality occurs only once in two days, may enable the parent to see the behaviour as less overwhelming, in the context of the rest of the time (the majority) spent in more positive interaction.

Even where such recording of the baseline is not in itself therapeutic it is necessary in order to identify whether the problematic behaviour improves. If it does, the recording of the improvement may itself be therapeutic and reinforce positive change. For example, star charts for children operate on the principle that an observed and recorded decline in problematic behaviour accompanied by parental praise, will reinforce continued more acceptable behaviour.

A second aspect of baseline diary-keeping is for the client to record what precedes the problematic behaviour and what follows it: in behavioural terms what is the stimulus to which such a behaviour is a response and what reinforces the behaviour. For example, such a diary might show that a child's temper tantrums were generally preceded by his baby sibling waking up, or it might show that they were reinforced by being given a sweet, by parental attention, or by being allowed to stay up later. This sequence is known as the *ABC* of a behavioural approach (Coulshed, 1988). *A* is the antecedent, *B* the behaviour and *C* the consequence. When they are recorded in detail worker and client may begin to identify the components most amenable to change, e.g. not rewarding problematic behaviour by sweets or attention.

In cognitive work not only are behaviour and its antecedents and consequences recorded but also the client's feelings and interpretations.

According to Dryden and Scott (1991) the cognitive model suggests that 'people are less disturbed by events in themselves and more by the way they view events' (p.177). In the cognitive approach *A* is the antecedent or stimulus, *B* the interpretation or evaluation of the event and *C* the emotional response. A client will therefore be asked to record not only behaviours but 'events between sessions they experience as upsetting. These may be external events (or interpretation of events) such as being criticised by a spouse, or internal events ...' (Dryden and Scott 1991, p. 178). Again the recording in itself may be therapeutic. Clients are also asked to identify and record 'what they might have said to themselves to get so upset, i.e. to find the *B*s of the *ABC* model'. Clients are thus helped to begin to recognise any pattern of interpretation which is self-destructive and the worker may be able, from the recording, to identify and challenge such a pattern.

We can also use written techniques to identify alternative responses and behaviours. Hall and Lloyd (1989) suggest an exercise to help women become more assertive but which could be adapted for other desired behaviour change. The exercise runs as follows:

Think of a situation you do not handle assertively which you would like to change and fill in the sheet below

- Situation/action/words of other person;
- My response;
- My feelings;
- What I wanted to say;
- How I would have chosen to handle the situation assertively.

Dealing with the past

Some pencil-and-paper tasks may be useful not just in assessment but in helping a client to understand the relevance of the past and perhaps lay some ghosts.

Life snakes or lifelines

This is a line drawn on paper to represent someone's life or part of life. Priestley *et al.* (1983) give the following instructions:

'Imagine that the 'snake' below represents your life. Starting from your childhood can you think of events, people or places that were turning-points for you? Mark these on the snake starting at the top. Also mark in things that were important to you at different times and show how these led to where you are now'.

So my snake might begin like Figure 9.1.

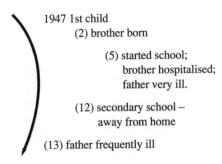

1947 1st child
    (2) brother born

        (5) started school;
            brother hospitalised;
            father very ill.

        (12) secondary school –
            away from home

    (13) father frequently ill

Figure 9.1

For an adult, drawing out a life history in such a way may show more clearly than verbal discussion the impact of past events or 'patterns' of events or behaviour previously unrecognised. For example, the pattern of illness in my male relatives in my childhood, emerges clearly.

For children, snakes may be a means by which worker and child try to find out and make sense of the child's history and to acknowledge breaks and discontinuities in care and relationships. They can provide a simple, pictorial alternative to the use of life-story books (Fahlberg, 1981) although for children in care with complex histories a life-story book may be a means of doing greater justice to the child's past and may be necessary in order for the child to have the kind of tangible history (photos, mementos, memories) usually held by parents.

Genograms

Genograms (see Figure 9.2) are like family trees and can fulfil a similar function to snakes in helping family members to understand past events in their history and to see 'patterns' of events or behaviour previously unrecognised. They can be done by children and may help them to

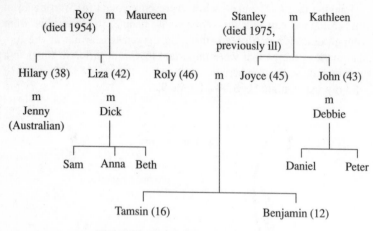

Figure 9.2   *Genogram of Lishman family*

communicate with their parents about aspects of family relationships they have not known or were confused about. Genograms usually start with children of the current family, working from the bottom of the page up. Family members are invited to discuss and write down salient issues as they arise in drawing the genogram.

Family trees or genograms become quite complicated. The finished product is not an end in itself but may help a family to communicate better about the past and understand its significance. For example, in my children's genogram, the premature death of their paternal grandfather whom they never met, had a profound influence on my son who was anxious that the same might happen to his father. Genograms, by putting complex family history in writing in one place, can help families to make connections and understand the significance of patterns of behaviour which continue to influence them, e.g. absent men, dominant women, even where all the individual bits were known and remembered by individual family members.

Life-story books

Fahlberg (1981) sees the life-story book as 'an opportunity to identify strong feelings about past events, to resolve issues, to correct misperceptions'. This seems to me a useful definition of purpose for each of the written techniques identified in Chapter 6, as ways of exploring and understanding clients' personal, family and social histories.

Fahlberg (1981) specifies further the purposes of the life-story book: it can help a child:

- to organise past events in the chronological schema;
- to aid ego development;
- to increase self-esteem;
- to re-read at her or his own pace;
- to share in orderly fashion her or his past with selected others;
- to build a sense of trust in the worker who aids in compiling the book;
- to gain acceptance of all facets of the child's life and to help the child accept his or her own past;
- to facilitate bonding (see Aldgate, 1991).

Again these purposes seem equally applicable to other written forms of exploring the past. Writing down a history makes it more tangible and identifies themes. Common themes which emerge for clients, children and adults, are of discrimination, rejection, deprivation, loss, stigma and abuse. Listening to and recording such histories can be painful in the extreme and the worker has to be trustworthy, sensitive and empathic and take time to explore with the client the thoughts and feelings which arise. A major issue for some clients is what to do with these feelings from the past: if an abusing father is dead he cannot be challenged and he cannot accept responsibility. For some clients, identifying the feelings, verbalising them, understanding where they come from and having them accepted by a trusted worker may be enough. Writing them down (see next section on dealing with feelings) may be useful.

Writing down a history identifies gaps more clearly than oral accounts where some bits get lost in the telling anyway. It may be possible to find the information from other family members or it may be lost: such a loss of history almost has to be grieved before it can be accepted.

Writing down a history identifies distortion and misperceptions e.g. a child may have thought he was unwanted. The history reveals his mother was ill and had to go into hospital so he was put into foster care. While the child/adult may question why no other family member was able to take him, and why this was never explained, his mother's concern to have him adequately cared for was not rejection and this misperception can usefully be clarified.

Finally, for an adult to construct his or her own written history enables her or him to experience some of the feelings which accompanied the original events and heightens the person's awareness of childhood feelings. My experience is that often adults need to grieve over painful childhood experiences, e.g. of inadequate parenting or rejection and the losses involved. Written histories can be a means to begin this process: experiencing the anger and sadness of their losses and the way they were (mis)treated can help adults to resolve some of their childhood pain, to accept some of their past and to be freer of the burden of this pain in adult life.

Dealing with feelings

Lists, diaries and letters are written techniques which aid exploration and expression of feelings.

Lists

While checklists have already been discussed, here a client is asked to generate his/her own list. Hall and Lloyd (1989, p.228) suggest it can be helpful to ask a woman who has suffered abuse:

- to write down a list of all the ways in which she is still affected by the abuse;
- to write down the ways she coped with the abuse as a child;
- to write down how she feels she has come to terms with the abuse since coming for help. The list should include her achievements and successes as well as any difficulties;
- to make a list of all the things she did right today;
- to write down what she has done to make herself feel better.

Clearly the latter lists are relevant to clients other than victims of abuse but Hall and Lloyd remind us of the difficulty that women who have been abused (or have low self-esteem for other reasons) have in appreciating and acknowledging their strengths. Many find writing a list of problems or weaknesses much easier. For them, to insist on a list of strengths or achievements may be the beginning of challenging their negative self-image.

For clients who have difficulty in acknowledging their anger, I have found that writing a list of 'things that make me angry' can help them to feel safer in expressing such anger than they would do in verbalising it. Similarly for some clients a list of 'things that make me sad' or 'anxious' may be the beginning of identifying and managing such painful feelings.

Diaries

Diaries and logs have also already been considered in relation to providing baselines of problematic behaviour and monitoring cognitive and behavioural changes. Hall and Lloyd (1989) see other functions of diaries; enhancing self-expression and empowerment, acknowledging change and development and identifying issues which have been dealt with and those which still recur.

Thus diaries can provide a useful record of the helping process including:

- expectations of a session or meeting;
- good or bad experiences during sessions;
- new memories;
- connections with the past made during sessions;
- reflections on relationships past and present (Hall and Lloyd, 1989, p. 231).

Such a record of thoughts and feelings, like life snakes and genograms acknowledges and makes concrete and real issues from the past or from current therapeutic work, whereas thoughts come and go and can be forgotten.

Letters

Letters also allow expression of difficult feelings. Hall and Lloyd (1989) suggest: 'Incest survivors can find it very helpful to write letters to significant people from their childhood. It allows them to express feelings which they might never have the courage to express verbally' (p.229). It also allows them to express feelings to someone who is dead or to someone they feel will be unable to respond. Again Hall and

Lloyd are referring specifically to women who have been abused, but writing a letter can be cathartic and therapeutic for someone who:

- experienced their parenting as unloving, unresponsive, or unreliable;
- has difficulty in confronting or expressing anger verbally;
- finds it difficult communicating verbally about feeling, with a parent, child, or partner;
- has unresolved feelings about someone who is dead.

I sometimes ask 'What would you like to say to X?' (parent or spouse, dead or alive). 'Write it down in a letter.' This letter does not have to be sent. Often the process of putting angry or painful feelings out on paper is enough and the letter is then consigned to the bin. If written to a dead parent, it may be thrown on the grave. Sometimes it may actually be given to parent or spouse, and, in conflict, a letter may have value. It can be read slowly, with time to try to understand the underlying message, rather than be responded to immediately or defensively, in the heat of an angry confrontation. Even where a letter is not understood, it may help the writer to come to terms with the lack of understanding and to move on to accept that the desired responses will never come but should not govern the rest of the writer's life and relationships.

Drawing

For children, drawing may be a way of expressing and trying to deal with complex and difficult feelings. A child whose parents were emotionally estranged drew a picture of each on the edge of a cliff, distant from each other but holding out a hand towards the other. A child whose sister had died drew a picture of a car crash and an ambulance: he talked about the picture, about going to hospital and about dying (as his sister had done). The worker commented that that sounded like his sister and that it seemed very frightening. The boy looked relieved, nodded and stopped drawing. Enough had been said for the time being.

As workers we can use particular techniques to explore and discuss feelings and relationships with children. We can draw faces and for each family member ask the child whether it should be a happy or a sad face. We can then explore why in the child's view each person is happy or sad. What would make a sad person happy? We can use sad and happy faces for a child in different care situations. Where was he happy/where sad? We can ask a child to draw his or her house and who lives there. This can be a way of exploring family relationships and problems from the child's point of view. Who is close to whom, who fights with whom? Are mother and father both there? Are other members of the extended family included? It can also be a useful means of exploring the child's world when abuse is suspected. We can ask what happens in each room: how easy and open is the child in doing this task? Is there any room which seems to cause anxiety, tension, apprehension or out-of-character refusal to speak? Here we may probe a little more specifically: who is usually in this room? Is it the child? Is it scary? Without being inquisitional, the use of drawing may help a child express forbidden or frightening anxieties, feelings or experiences, although again the adult with whom this is done has to be perceived as trustworthy.

Finally we can play squiggles (Winnicott, 1971) with a child or adolescent. Wardle (1975) describes its application to social work with children 'The game is played between a "helping" adult and child. Person *A* draws a random squiggle which Person *B* turns into a picture; then vice versa. The value is that a child may quickly relax and become interested in the game; he may soon start drawing the whole picture himself, perhaps more freely and happily than if asked by a fairly unknown person "to draw whatever you like". Perhaps the most important feature is that it is shared.' Squiggles can be just a game, but they can be a means for a child to draw and communicate themes and issues which are important for her or him.

Chapters 8 and 9 have examined non-verbal, verbal and written communication skills and techniques which may be used to help clients to solve problems and change attitudes or behaviour. They have emphasised that to do this the worker is engaged in influencing the client, and they have focused on specific skills and techniques rather than broader models of intervention. However, we should also be aware that one of the ways in which we may implicitly influence clients is by modelling. Fischer (1978) says, 'Modelling refers simply to a change in behaviour as a result of the observation of another's behaviour, i.e. learning by vicarious experience or imitation'(p.169). Modelling is used consciously as one technique in behaviour modification: here a worker 'repeatedly demonstrates desired responses, instructs the client to reproduce them, prompts the behaviour when it fails to occur and administer potent reinforcers to the client' (Fischer, 1978, p.169).

However, Fischer also argues that increasing evidence that behaviour can be learned through observation of the behaviour of others suggests that 'it is likely that a good deal of "everyday learning" takes place through modelling' (p.169). Bandura (1977) also suggests that the effectiveness of modelling is enhanced if:

- the model has some standing (e.g. power, attractiveness or relationship) in the eyes of the subject;
- there is some similarity between the model and the subject so the subject does not feel it is impossible to achieve similar behaviour to the subject.

We have noted that clients themselves appreciate workers having 'some standing' (relationship skills, authority or expertise) and some interests in common with clients.

If these conditions are met and we establish both a relationship base and an influence base it is at least possible that some of our communication and behaviour acts as a model for clients even if we do not consciously seek this. The use of communication skills examined in this book may therefore fulfil two functions for clients: to facilitate them in dealing more effectively with their problems and to model behaviours and communication skills which in themselves may increase problem-solving abilities.

10

Conclusion

I hope this book has introduced the reader to a range of communication skills which underlie effective social work practice. It can only be an introduction. Skills have to be practised and developed on the basis of feedback from clients, colleagues, or, in training, from peers, tutors and video. I hope, however, that this book challenges readers to reflect on and examine their own practice, raises their awareness of their skills and weaknesses in communication and encourages them to action: to practise, improve, extend and develop their communication skills.

The skills involved in attending and listening, engaging and relating, giving and getting information, negotiating agreements or contracts and helping people to make changes in their attitudes, beliefs or behaviour are relevant to social work in all contexts. Each context will influence the way in which communication occurs, both enhancing and encouraging the use of some skills and constraining or limiting the use of others.

In group or residential care the skills of attending and listening, of sharing information, of agreeing shared goals and targets for change, and of clarification, interpretation and challenging are employed in the context of daily living rather than in a formal time-limited interview. The concept of the life space is relevant, defined by Keenan (1991) as a 'therapeutic and institutional environment wherein residents or attenders enact both existential and historical aspects of their lives in the context of relations with each other, professional and other staff, their systems and subsystems' (p.220). Within the life space the daily patterns of residential or group care, washing-up, meals, bedtime, offer the opportunity at times for purposeful and meaningful communication.

Much of the communication in residential or group care is the everyday stuff of normal living, but sometimes the communication has a significance for the resident or user which the worker has to pick up and respond to. This requires the worker to understand the meaning underlying the interaction and to communicate that understanding. An adolescent boy was particularly abusive to a young Scots male care-worker. It emerged, coincidentally, that his mother was just about to marry a much younger man, a Scot. The residential worker took time to explore the boy's feelings and to reflect back the link between his aggressive behaviour in care and his anger about his new stepfather. The capacity to respond appropriately depends not just on the worker's communication skills, but also on the constraints of the setting, including difficulties about privacy and the needs and demands of other residents or users.

The context also constrains communication in social work in secondary settings. If an interview has to be conducted at the patient's bedside in a public ward, privacy is impossible and the patient/client may well feel inhibited from sharing real concerns or feelings e.g. of anxiety, distress or anger, because of the public nature of the setting. Interruptions are also frequent and can inhibit real communication. I became particularly aware of the impact of interruptions when I was sitting in a cubicle with a terminally ill child and his parents. He was asleep and they were preparing for his death, partly by talking about the practical arrangements for his funeral, partly by sitting silently and partly by grieving openly. They needed peace and privacy but ward routines continued and there were frequent interruptions to check the child's condition.

Referrals to social work in secondary settings are often by a third party, e.g. a nurse, doctor or headmaster, and can be made without the knowledge of the person referred (Woodhouse, 1987). It is, therefore, essential for the social worker to clarify whether the person knows about the referral or wishes for social-work contact. The skills of engagement, clarification of purpose, giving information about the role and resources of social work, and negotiation of a mutually agreed contract are essential for a social worker practising in a secondary setting.

Finally, the very nature of a secondary setting may constrain effective social-work communication because the primary purpose of the organisation is not the practice of social work. The priorities, values, professional beliefs and ideologies of the different disciplines involved will vary. Because of its lack of relative status and power, social work is unlikely to be in a position to assert and achieve the primacy of its beliefs and values, although individual social workers may achieve personal influence within their multidisciplinary teams.

The conflict in professional beliefs can constrain both the social-work role and communication between worker and client. For example, social workers in psychiatric hospitals may be viewed by nursing and medical colleagues only in terms of their mental health officer role, or of their

welfare rights expertise. Nursing and medical staff may show disapproval of the social worker for 'upsetting' the patient if the social worker's appropriate use of listening, probing, empathy and reflection results
in a patient sharing distress.

Fieldwork settings provide their own constraints, some of which have
already been discussed, for example, the power and authority of the
social worker, or whether the client is seen on a voluntary or statutory
basis, although the issue of power is highlighted when the basis of the
contract is a legal requirement. In child care, particularly, social workers
operate within the constraint of the clients' fear of their power to
remove children into care.

The physical setting of fieldwork may interfere with effective communication. An office is not a client's natural setting, but rather an alien
and artificial one. It is the social worker's territory, not the client's, and
therefore the social worker retains control. It conveys professional
power, authority and distance reminiscent of other offices and interviews, with GPs, lawyers or DHSS officials.

Perhaps the main constraint on communication in fieldwork is the time
limit. In contrast to residential or group care, a fieldwork interview is a
brief episode in a client's life: used for assessment it is inevitably limited,
a snapshot of what a client is prepared to reveal. Even a more regular
contact, for example, on a weekly basis, has to be seen in the context of
the client's other relationships, commitments and networks. Inevitably
there are severe limitations on the influence of a social worker's hour-a-
week contact with a client, set in the context of the complexity of the rest
of the client's life, including immediate family, social networks and,
most influential of all, structural position in society. In particular, as the
introduction acknowledged, an individual social worker's communication skills can do little to address the structural problems of poverty,
class, gender and race which face many of social work's clients.

In concluding any book, the author has to examine and review critically its content and omissions. I am particularly aware of two problems
in this volume. First, as I indicated in the introduction, writing about
communication cannot do it justice. Communication is an activity: it has
to be practised, reviewed and thereby improved in order to do it effectively. This book can only be a tool and an impetus, and not, in itself, a
means to effective communication. Second, it is difficult to do justice to
the diversity of social work, its settings, its client groups, its purposes
and aims, and its individual clients in relation to their class, gender,
ethnicity, age and personality. In particular, the analysis of communica-

tion and culture is limited. I have only been able to highlight key issues: dealing with them in depth would require a separate volume. Third, the focus of this book has been about communicating with clients. However the skills involved are just as relevant and necessary to effective communication with colleagues both from social work and from other professions, disciplines and occupations.

Within these limitations, what are the requirements of effective communication in social work?

First, it requires the development and use of a range of skills and techniques examined in this book:

- engaging and establishing rapport;
- attentive listening to the meaning of the clients' communication;
- exploration, questioning and probing;
- summarising and focusing;
- establishing a shared purpose, mutually agreed between the client and the worker;
- giving information or advice;
- reflection and clarification;
- challenging and confrontation.

These are the technical components of effective communication. Without the knowledge or ability to practise this repertoire of skills, the social worker is unlikely to use encounters with clients for purposeful communication.

Such technical expertise is necessary for effective communication in social work, but is not enough. Social work involves entering into the lives of people who are in distress, conflict or trouble. To do this requires not only technical competence, but also qualities of integrity, genuineness and self-awareness.

Social workers have to begin from a value base which entails basic respect for all human beings. While I recognise that individual clients may be dishonest, destructive or dangerous, social work has to start from humanistic principles or values about the worth and dignity of each individual. Social workers also need to possess the Rogerian qualities of genuineness and authenticity. If we are not honest and authentic and real in our practice the skills outlined in this volume become hollow and mechanistic. Skills have to be based on integrity. In part this is a moral consideration: it represents my belief that the vulnerability of clients requires a personal response and commitment from me as a person, as well as my professional technical competence. It is also an empirical issue: client studies and the evaluation of counselling have highlighted genuineness or authenticity as a necessary, but not sufficient, condition of effective helping.

The final requirement for effective communication is the worker's self-awareness. Communication, verbal, non-verbal or symbolic, is about our use of self. In order to communicate effectively we have to be aware of what we are doing, why we are doing it, how we are presenting ourselves to our clients, and, on the basis of this self-knowledge or awareness, what changes in our communication are needed if we are to be more effective.

Skilled and effective communication is not a static state. It will always involve change and development and consolidation, learning from our past behaviour and from our mistakes. I hope this book stimulates and challenges its readers to do just that: to learn, to develop and to consolidate their communication skills.

References

Aldgate, J. (1991) 'Attachment Theory and its Application to Child Care Social Work', in Lishman (1991).

American Bar Association (1980) *Probation* (approved draft), Project on Standards for Criminal Justice, New York, Institute of Judicial Administration.

Anon. (1973) 'Another Sleepless Night: A Parent's Viewpoint', *Social Work*, 18(1) January, pp. 112–114

Argyle, M. (1972) *The Psychology of Interpersonal Behaviour*, Harmondsworth, Penguin.

Argyle, M. (1973) *Social Interaction*, London, Tavistock.

Argyle, M. (1975) 'Non-Verbal Communication', in M.Brown and R. Stevens (eds) *Social Behaviour and Experience: Multiple Perspectives*, London, Open University Press.

Argyle, M. (1978) *Social Encounter: Readings in Social Interaction*, Harmondsworth, Penguin.

Argyle, M. Salter, V., Nicholson, H. and Burgess, P. (1970) 'The Communication of Inferior and Superior Attitudes by Verbal and Non-Verbal Signals', *British Journal of Social and Clinical Psychology*, vol. 9, pp. 221–31.

Baldock, J. Prior, D. (1981) 'Social Workers Talking to Clients: A Study of Verbal Behaviour', *British Journal of Social Work*, vol. 11, No 1.

Bandura, A. (1977) *Social Learning Theory*, Englewood Cliffs, NJ: Prentice Hall.

Barker, P.J. (1975) 'Clients' Likes and Dislikes', *Social Work Today,* vol. 6, no 3, pp. 77–8.

Becker, S. Macpherson, S. (1988) *Public Issues and Private Pain: Poverty, Social Work and Social Policy*, London, Social Services Insight Books.

Bedfordshire Social Services Department (1978) *Handicapped Children.*

Berenson, B.G. Mitchell, K.M. (1974) *Confrontation: For Better or Worse*, Amherst, Massachusetts, Human Resource Development Press.

Berne, E. (1964) *Games People Play*, New York, Grove Press.

Berry, J. (1971) 'Helping Children Directly', *British Journal of Social Work*, vol. 1, no 3.

Biestek, F.P. (1965) *The Casework Relationship*, London, Unwin University Books.

Blaxter, M. (1976) *The Meaning of Disability*, London, Heinemann.

Booth, T. (1983) 'Residents' Views, Rights and Institutional Care', in M. Fisher (ed) *Speaking of Clients,* Sheffield, Social Services Monographs: Research in Practice; Community Care and University of Sheffield Joint Unit for Social Services Research.

Bottoms, A., and Stellman, A. (1988) *Social Inquiry Reports*, Wildwood House, Hampshire, Community Care Practice Handbooks.

Bowlby, J. (1984) *The Making and Breaking of Affectional Bonds*, London, Tavistock, Social Science Paperbacks.

Brackbill, Y. (1958) 'Extinction of the Smiling Response in Infants as a Function of Reinforcement Schedule', *Child Development*, vol. 29, pp. 115–24

Brammer, L. (1973) *The Helping Relationship: Process and Skills*, Englewood Cliffs, New Jersey, Prentice-Hall.

Breakwell, G.M. and Rowett, C. (1982) *Social Work: the Social Psychological Approach*, Wokingham, Berkshire, Van Nostrand Reinhold (UK).

Burnham, J.B. (1986) *Family Therapy: First Steps towards a Systemic Approach*, London, Tavistock.

Butler, N. (1977) 'Uncovering a Gap in the Service', *Community Care*, vol. 3, August, pp. 14–16.

Byrne, P.S and Long, B.E.L. (1976) *Doctors talking to Patients: A Study of the Verbal Behaviour of General Practitioners Consulting in their Surgeries*, London, HMSO/DHSS.

Carew, R. (1979) 'The Place of Knowledge in Social Work Activity', *British Journal of Social Work*, vol. 9.

Carkhuff, R.R. (1969) *Helping and Human Relations*, New York, Holt.

CCETSW (1975) *Education and Training for Social Work*, London Central Council for Education and Training in Social Work, Paper 10.

CCETSW (Scotland) (1992) *Training for Social Work Practice in the Criminal Justice System*, Edinburgh, Guidance for DipSW programme providers in Scotland.

Clark, D. and Haldane, D. (1990) *Wedlocked: Intervention and Research in Marriage*, Cambridge, England, Polity Press

Clough, R. (1982) *Residential Work*, Basingstoke, Macmillan.

Cohen, A. (1971) 'Consumer View: Retarded Mothers and the Social Services', *Social Work Today*, vol. 1, pp. 35–43

Collins, J.A. (1977) 'A Contractual Guide to Social Work Intervention', *Social Work Today*, vol. 8.

Cook, M. (1968) *Studies of Orientation and Proximity*, Oxford, Institute of Experimental Psychology.

Corden, John (1980) 'Contracts in Social Work Practice', *British Journal of Social Work*, vol. 10, pp. 143–61.

Corden, J. and Preston-Short, M. (1987) 'Contract or Con Trick? A Reply to Rojek and Collins', *British Journal of Social Work*, vol. 17, pp. 535–43.

Coulshed, V. (1988) *Social Work Practice: An Introduction*, Basingstoke, Macmillan/BASW.

Criminal Justice (Scotland) Act 1949.

Dale, P., Davies, M., Morrison, T. and Waters, J. (1986) *Dangerous Families: Assessment and Treatment of Child Abuse*, London, Tavistock.

Daly, M.J. and Burton, R.L. (1983) 'Self-esteem and Irrational Beliefs: An Exploratory Investigation with Implications for Counselling', *Journal of Counselling Psychology*, vol. 23.

D'Ardenne, P. and Mahtani, A. (1989) *Transcultural Counselling in Action*, London, Sage.

Davies, M. (1985) *The Essential Social Worker*, Aldershot, Gower/Community Care.

Davis, L.F. (1989) *Senses and Sensibility in Child Care: Concerns and Conflicts*, London, Open University/Hodder & Stoughton.

DHSS (1974) *Report of the Inquiry into the Care and Supervision provided in relation to Maria Coldwell*, London HMSO.

Doel, M. and Lawson, B. (1986) 'Open Records: The Client's Right to Partnership', *British Journal of Social Work*, vol, 16, pp. 407–30.

Dryden, W. and Scott, M. (1991) 'A Brief, Highly Structured and Effective Approach to Social Work Practice: A Cognitive–Behavioural Perspective', in Lishman (1991).

Egan, G. (1986) *The Skilled Helper: A Systematic Approach to Effective Helping*, Monterey, California, Brooks/Coles.

Eisenthal, S. and Lazare, A. (1976) 'Evaluation of the Initial Interview in a Walk-in Clinic (the patient's perspective on a "customer approach")', *Journal of Nervous and Mental Diseases* , vol. 162, pp. 169–70.

Ekman, P. Friesan, W.V. (1968) 'Non-verbal Behaviour in Psychotherapy Research', in J.M. Schlien (ed.) *Research in Psychotherapy*, 3, Washington, DC, American Psychological Association.

Ellis, A. (1962) *Reason and Emotion in Psychotherapy*, New York, Lyle Stuart.

Exline, R.V. (1963) 'Explorations in the Process of Person Perception: Visual Interaction in Relation to Competition, Sex and the Need for "Affiliation" ', *Journal of Personality*, vol. 31, pp. 1–20.

Exline, R.V. and Winters, L.C. (1965) 'Affective Relations and Mutual Glances in Dyads', in S. Tomkins and C. Izzard (eds) *Affect, Cognition and Personality*, New York, Springer.

Fahlberg, V. (1981) *Helping Children When They Must Move*, London, British Agencies Adoption and Fostering.

Fischer, J. (1978) *Effective Casework: An Eclectic Approach*, New York, McGraw-Hill.

Fisher, M., Marsh, P. and Philip, D. with Sainsbury, E. (1986) *In and Out of Care,* London, Batsford.

Frank, J.D. (1973) *Persuasion and Healing,* Baltimore, Johns Hopkins University Press, 2nd edn.

Freeman, I. and Montgomery, S. (1988) *Child Care: Monitoring Practice,* London, Jessica Kingsley, Research Highlights in Social Work 17.

Furnham, A. and Bochner, S. (1986) *Culture Shock: Psychological Reaction to Unfamiliar Environments*, London, Methuen.

Gandy, J.M., Pitman, R., Stretcher, M. and Yip, C. (1975) Parents' Perception of the Effect of Volunteer Probation Officers in Juvenile Offenders', *Canadian Journal of Criminology and Corrections*, vol. 17, pp. 5–19.

George, V. and Wilding, R. (1972) *Motherless Families*, London, Routledge and Kegan Paul.

Glampson, A. and Goldberg, E.M. (1976) 'Post-Seebohm Services (2) from the Consumers' Viewpoint', *Social Work Today*, vol. 8, 9 November.

Goldberg, E.M. (1981) 'Monitoring in the Social Services' in Goldberg and Connelly (1981).

Goldberg, E.M. and Connelly, N. (eds) 1981 *Evaluative Research in Social Care,* London, Heinemann.

Goldberg, E.M., Walker, D. and Robinson, J. (1977) 'Exploring the Task-centred Casework Method', *Social Work Today*, vol. 9, 6 September 1977.

Goldberg, E.M. and Warburton, R.W. (1979) *Ends and Means in Social Work*, London, Allen & Unwin.

Gorell Barnes, G. (1984) *Working with Families*, Basingstoke, Macmillan.

Gottesfeld, H. (1965) 'Professionals and Delinquents Evaluate Professional Methods with Delinquents', *Social Problems*, vol. 13.

Grampian Regional Council: Grampian Health Board (1991) *Draft Joint Community Care Plan*, March 1991.

Greenspoon, J. (1955) 'The Reinforcing Effect of Two Spoken Sounds on the Frequency of Two Responses', *American Journal of Psychology*, vol. 68.

Gurin, G., Keroft, J. and Feld, S. (1960) *Americans View their Mental Health*, New York Basic Books.

Gurney, M. (1990) 'Anxiety Overload', *Community Care*, 15 November.

Hall, A.S. (1974) *The Point of Entry*, London, Allen and Unwin.

Hall, L. and Lloyd, S. (1989) *Surviving Child Sexual Abuse: A Handbook for Helping Women Challenge their Past*, London, Falmer Press.

Hamilton, Gordon (1951) *Theory and Practice of Social Casework*, New York, Columbia University Press.

Hargie, O. (1986) *A Handbook of Communication Skills*, London and Sydney, Croom Helm.

Hargie, O., Tittmer, H and Dickson, D. (1978) '"Microtraining": A Systematic Approach to Social Work Practice' , *Social Work Today*, vol. 9, 18 April 1978.

Henley, A. (1979) *Asian Parents in Hospitals and at Home*, London, King Edward's Hospital Fund.

Hoffman, W.P.F. (1975) *Expectations of Mental Health Centre Clients related to Problem Reductions and Satisfaction with Services*, University of Pennsylvania Department of Social Work, summary from *Abstracts for Social Workers*, vol. 11(3), no. 700.

Hollis, F. (1967) 'Explorations in the Development of a Typology of Casework', *Social Casework*, vol. 48.

Howe, D. (1980) 'Inflated States and Empty Theories in Social Work', *British Journal of Social Work*, vol. 10.

Hudson, B. (1991) 'Behavioural Social Work', in Lishman (1991).

Jackson, F. (1973) 'Families and workers in Islington', *Islington Family Services Unit Quarterly*, vol. 5.

Kadushin, A. (1990) *The Social Work Interview: A Guide for Human Service Professionals*, New York, Columbia University Press.

Katz, D. and Braly, K. (1933) 'Racial Stereotypes of One Hundred College Students', *Journal of Abnormal and Social Psychology*, vol. 28, pp. 280–90

Keenan, C. (1991) 'Working within the Life Space' in Lishman (1991).

Kendon, A. (1973) 'Some Functions of Gaze-Direction in Social Interaction', in M. Argyle (ed.) *Social Encounters: Readings in Social Interaction*, Harmondsworth, Penguin.

Langan, M. and Lee, P. (1989) *Radical Social Work Today*, London, Unwin Hyman.

Ley, P. (1977) 'Communicating with the Patient', in J.C. Coleman (ed.) *Introductory Psychology*, London, Routledge & Kegan Paul.

Lishman, J. (1978) 'A Clash in Perspective', *British Journal of Social Work*, Autumn, pp. 301–11.

Lishman, J. (ed.) (1984) *Evaluation*, London, Jessica Kingsley, Research Highlights in Social Work 8.

Lishman, J. (1985) 'An Analysis of Social Work Interviews using Videotapes: Behaviour, Effectiveness and Self-fulfilling Prophecies', University of Aberdeen, PhD thesis.

Lishman, J. (ed.) (1991) *Handbook of Theory for Practice Teachers in Social Work*, London, Jessica Kingsley.

Lishman, J., Macintosh, L. and Macintosh, B. (1990) 'A Child Dies', *Practice*, Autumn/Winter, pp. 271–84.

Lott, R.E., Clark, W. and Altman, I. (1969) *A Propositional Inventory of Research on Interpersonal Space*, Washington, Naval Medical Research Institute.

Maluccio, A. and Marlow, W.D. (1974) 'The Case for Contract', *Social Work (USA)*, vol. 19.

Maluccio, A.N. (1979) *Learning from Clients: Interpersonal Helping Viewed by Clients and Social Workers*, New York, Free Press.

Marris, P. (1974) *Loss and Change*, London, Routledge & Kegan Paul.

Marsh, P. (1991) 'Task-centred Casework' in Lishman (1991).

Mayer, J.E. and Timms, N. (1970) *The Client Speaks*, London, Routledge and Kegan Paul.

Mehrabian, A. (1972) *Non-verbal Communication*, Alberta, Aldine.

Mehrabian, A. and Williams, H. (1969) 'Non-verbal Concomitants of Perceived and Extended Persuasiveness', *Journal of Personality and Social Psychology*, vol. 13.

Miller, R.L., Brickman, P. and Boch, D. (1975) 'Attribution versus Persuasion as a Means of Modifying Behaviour', *Journal of Personality and Social Psychology*, vol. 31.

Milner, J. (1982) 'A Myth Dispelled', *Community Care*, 4 February 1982.

Mullen, E. (1968) 'Casework Communication', *Social Casework*, vol. 49.

Nelson-Jones, R. (1983) *Practical Counselling Skills*, Eastbourne, Holt, Rinehart and Winston.

Neville, D. and Beak, D. (1990) 'Solving the Case History Mystery', *Social Work Today*, 28 June 1990.

Newcombe, T.M. (1961) *The Acquaintance Process*, London, Holt.

Nicolson, P. and Bayne, R. (1984) *Applied Psychology for Social Workers*, Basingstoke, Macmillan.

O'Hagan, K. (1986) *Crisis Intervention in Social Services*, Basingstoke, Macmillan.

O'Hagan, K. (1991) 'Crisis Intervention in Social Work' in Lishman (1991).

Oliver, J. (1990) 'The Customers' Perspective Campaign: Reception Areas', *Social Work Today*, 5 April 1990.

Orlinsky, D.E. and Howard, J.K. (1967) 'The Good Therapy Hour: Experimental Correlates of Patients' and Therapists' Evaluations of Therapy Sessions', *Archive of General Psychology*, vol. 16, pp. 621–32.

Orlinsky, D.E. and Howard, K.I. (1978) 'The Relation of Process to Outcome in Psychotherapy', in A.E. Burgin and S.L. Garfield (eds) *Handbook of Psychotherapy and Behaviour Change*, New York, Wiley, 2nd edn.

Ovretveit, J. (1986) *Improving Social Work Records and Practice*, London, British Association of Social Workers.

Parkes, C.M. (1975) *Bereavement*, Harmondsworth, Pelican.

Payne, M. (1978) 'Uses of Social Work Records', *Social Work Today*, vol. 9, pp. 254–78.

Payne, M. (1991) *Modern Social Work Theory: A Critical Introduction,* Basingstoke, Macmillan.

Pease, K. (1983) *Penal Innovations*, London, Jessica Kingsley, Research Highlights 5, Social Work with Adult Offenders.

Perlman, H. (1957) *Social Casework: a Problem-Solving Process*, Chicago, Chicago, University Press.

Philipps, D. (1983) 'Mayer and Timms Revisited: the Evolution of Client Studies', in M. Fisher (ed.) *Speaking of Clients*, Sheffield, Community Care and University of Sheffield Joint Unit for Social Services Research, 1983.

Pincus, A. and Minahan, A. (1973) *Social Work Practice: Model and Method*, Itasca, Illinois, University of Wisconsin/Peacock Publishers Inc.

Pithouse, A. (1987) *Social Work: The Organisation of an Invisible Trade*, London, Gower.

Priestley, P. and McGuire, J. (1983) *Learning to Help: Basic Skills Exercises*, London, Tavistock.

Priestley, P., McGuire, J., Flegg, D., Helmsley, V. and Wellham, D. (1978) *Social Skills and Personal Problem Solving: A Handbook of Methods*, London, Tavistock.

Reece, M.M. and Whitman, R.N. (1962) 'Expressive Movements, Warmth and Verbal Reinforcements', *Journal of Abnormal and Social Psychology*, vol. 64.

Rees, S. and Wallace, A. (1982) *Verdicts on Social Work*, London, Edward Arnold.

Rees, S.J. (1974) 'No more than Contact: an Outcome of Social Work' *British Journal of Social Work*, vol. 4, pp. 255–79.

Rees, S.J. (1978) *Social Work Face to Face*, London, Edward Arnold

Reid, W. and Epstein, L. (1972) *Task Centred Casework*, New York, Columbia University Press.

Reid, W.J. (1967) 'Characteristics of Client Intervention', *Welfare in Review*, vol. 5.

Reid, W.J. and Hanrahan, P. (1981) 'The Effectiveness of Social Work: Recent Evidence', in Goldberg and Connelly, 1981.

Reid, W.J. and Shyne, A. (1969) *Brief and Extended Casework*, New York, Columbia University Press.

Reith, D. (1975) 'I wonder if you can help me?', *Social Work Today*, vol. 6.

Reith, D. (1988) 'Evaluation – A Function of Practice' in Lishman, (1988).

Rice, L.N. (1965) 'Therapists' Evaluative Statements and Patient Outcome in Psychotherapy', *Journal of Consulting Psychology*, vol. 29.

Robinson, T. (1978) *In Worlds Apart*, London, Bedford Square Press.

Rodgers, B.N. and Dixon, J. (1960) *Portrait of Social Work*, Oxford, Oxford University Press.

Rogers, C.R. (1957) 'The Necessary and Sufficient Conditions of Therapeutic Personality Change', *Journal of Consulting Psychology*, vol. 21.

Rogers, C.R. (1980) *A Way of Being*, Boston, Massachusetts, Houghton Mifflin.

Rogers, C.R, Shostrom, E. and Lazarus, A. (1977) *Three Approaches to Psychotherapy, II*, A film distributed by Psychological Films, Inc., Orange, California.

Rogers, C.R. and Truax, C.B. (1967) 'The Therapeutic Conditions Antecedent to Change: A Theoretical View', in C.R. Rogers (ed.) *The Therapeutic Relationship and its Impact*, Madison, Wisconsin, University of Wisconsin Press.

Rojek, C. and Collins, S.A. (1987) 'Contract or Con Trick?', *British Journal of Social Work*, vol. 17, pp. 199–211.

Sainsbury, E. (1975) *Social Work with Families*, London, Routledge & Kegan Paul.

Sainsbury, E. and Nixon, S. (1979) 'Organisational Influences on the Ways in which Social Work Practice is Perceived by Social Workers and Clients', unpublished first draft, University of Sheffield.

Sainsbury, E., Nixon. S. and Phillips, D. (1982) *Social Work in Focus*, London, Routledge & Kegan Paul.

Salmon, W. (1972) 'A Service Program in a State Public Welfare Agency', in Reid and Epstein (1972).

Schmidt, J. (1969) 'The Use of Purpose in Casework', *Social Work*, vol. 14.

Schwartz, W. (1973) 'Thoughts from Abroad: Some Perspectives on the Practice of Social Work', *Social Work Today*, vol. 14.

Selby, J.W. and Halhoun, L.G. (1980) 'Psychodidactics: An Undervalued and Underdeveloped Tool of Psychological Intervention', *Professional Psychology*, vol. 11, pp. 236–41.

Shackman, J. (1985) *A Handbook on Working with, Employing and Training Interpreters*, National Extension College, Cambridge.

Sheldon, B. (1977) 'Do You Know Where You're Going?', *Community Care*, 8 June 1977.

Sheldon, B. (1988) 'Single-case Evaluation Methods: Review and Prospects', in Lishman (1988).

Sheldon, B. and Baird, P. (1978) 'Evaluating Student Performance', *Social Work Today*, 10.

Silverman, P.R. (1969) 'The Client Who Drops Out: A Study of Spoiled Helping Relationships', Brandeis University, PhD thesis.

Smith, C.R. (1980) 'Adoption Policy and Practice', Leeds University, PhD thesis.

Smith, C.R. (1982) *Social Work with the Dying and the Bereaved*, Basingstoke, Macmillan.

Sommer, R. (1965) 'Further Studies of Small Group Ethology', *Sociometry*, vol. 28, pp. 337–48.

Streatfield Report (1961) 'Report of the Interdepartmental Committee on the Business of the Criminal Courts', London, HMSO, Cmnd 1289.

Strong, S.R. (1968) 'Counselling: An Interpersonal Influence Process', *Journal of Counselling Psychology*, vol. 30, pp. 557–65.

Sutton, C. (1979) *Psychology for Social Workers and Counsellors*, London, Routledge & Kegan Paul, Library of Social Work.

Swenson, C.H. (1973) *Introduction to Interpersonal Relations*, Glenview, Illinois, and Brighton, England, Scott Foresman & Co.

Truax, C,B. (1966) 'Reinforcement and Non-reinforcement in Rogerian Psychotherapy', *Journal of Abnormal and Social Psychology*, vol. 71.

Truax, C.B. and Carkhuff, R.R. (1957) 'Towards Effective Counselling and Psychotherapy', *Journal of Counselling Psychology*, vol. 21.

Vernon, P.E. (1964) *Personality Assessment*, London, Methuen.

Vickery, A. (1977) 'Social Casework', in H. Sprecht and A. Vickery (eds) *Integrating Social Work Methods*, London, Allen & Unwin.

Wallace, A. and Rees, S. (1988) 'The Priority of Client Evaluations', in Lishman (1988).

Wardle, M. (1975) 'Hippopotamus or Cow? On Not Communicating With Children', *Social Work Today*, vol. 6, 16 November 1975.

Weiss, R.S. (1972) 'Helping Relationships: Relationships of Clients with Physicians, Social Workers, Priests and Others', *Social Problems*, vol. 20, pp. 319–28

Winnicott, D.W. (1971) *Therapeutic Consultations in Child Psychiatry*, London, Hogarth Press.

Wolberg, L. (1954) *Techniques of Psychotherapy*, New York, Grune and Stratton.

Wood, K.M. (1978) 'Casework Effectiveness: A New Look at Research Evidence', *Social Work*, vol. 23, pp. 437–59.

Woodhouse, J. (1987) 'Towards an Easeful Death: Social Work with a Dying Man', in R. Harris (ed.) *Practising Social Work*, Leicester University, School of Social Work, Case Studies in Social Work Education.

Worby, M. (1953) 'The Adolescent's Expectation of How the Potentially Helpful Person will Act', *Smith College Studies in Social Work*, vol. 26, p. 59.

Index